The Flaw
in the Universe

Natural Disaster and Human Sin

First published by O-Books, 2010
O-Books is an imprint of John Hunt Publishing Ltd., The Bothy, Deershot Lodge, Park Lane, Ropley,
Hants, SO24 0BE, UK
office1@o-books.net
www.o-books.com

For distributor details and how to order please visit the 'Ordering' section on our website.

ISBN: 978 1 84694 344 7

Design: Stuart Davies

Printed in the UK by CPI Antony Rowe

O Books operates a distinctive and ethical publishing philosophy in
all areas of our business, from our global network of authors to
production and worldwide distribution.

The Flaw
in the Universe

Natural Disaster and Human Sin

Adrian Hough

BOOKS

Winchester, UK
Washington, USA

CONTENTS

To Kathryn and Rachel

Foreword

It is a natural human tendency to want to categorize, or system-atize, experience. Without categories or systems of knowledge there could be no thought and no understanding. Experience would consist of a profusion of unrelated impressions. So, science, theology, philosophy, history and aesthetics are all ways, among others, of attempting to render experience intelligible by systematically categorizing what we can know of the world around us from a particular perspective or through one particular prism of analysis and conceptual thought.

But what of the relationship of these different ways of knowing to one another? Are they mutually exclusive or contra-dictory; is it all a matter of choice and which system happens to speak best to us; and on what basis do we choose? Or are they complementary? What is the possibility of dialogue between them? And can the insights from one discipline not only cohere with those of another, and so help to affirm them, but might they also help each discipline to push its own boundaries and so be assisted in its development as a result?

Such questions as these are very much at the heart of this innovative and wide-ranging study, in which Adrian Hough explores some aspects of the relationship between science and theology through the unusual perspective of the Second Law of Thermodynamics and its resonance with the classical Christian doctrine of Original Sin. What emerges is no superficial synthesis but a genuine dialogue between two very creative systems of thought. Similarly whilst not being, in the strict sense, a work of Christian apologetics, nevertheless in the enterprise of bringing together in conversation two disciplines, each of which sets out to explain in its own way the world as it is, and how it impacts on the everyday experience of us all, there is inevitably an explo-ration of the presuppositions of each approach and its integrity or effectiveness as an intellectual enterprise.

To that extent this book, in inviting us to consider afresh some of the core doctrines of the Christian faith in a fresh and thought-provoking way, offers tools for a deeper understanding of the role of systematic theology in commending the Christian faith today. At the same time it makes an important contribution to enabling a mature debate between science and other approaches to human knowledge, at a time when much public discourse in this area is often simplistic, polarized and ill-informed. There is an elegance to the argument set out in these pages, and that in itself speaks of the breadth and depth of the enterprise covered in this fairly short compass.

This does mean that there are times when the reader of this book is made to work hard, but those who persevere will find that it is to good effect, with many resonances to a range of contemporary issues from the rise of earth system science amid concerns about the future of the planet, to some of the theological presuppositions that lay behind divisions in the Christian church. Those who approach this book from a theological perspective will find much here to challenge thinking about where and how the interface with other intellectual disciplines should be found. On the other hand, in the words of Adrian Hough himself, 'Atheistic reductionists may one day discover that the only place where their dream of being able to calculate everything from first principles is true is in the Kingdom of God!'

+ Michael Exon.
27 July 2009

Preface

One of the remarkable features of Christian theology throughout the past few decades has been the considerable growth in the interest which has been shown in the relationship between theology and science. In an age which is heavily dependent on the products of science and technology this is a subject which is highly relevant to the mission of the Christian church and it is encouraging that the interest appears to be continuing in the present day.

However, the nature of the relationship between theology and science is of considerable interest and importance not merely for its own sake, and for the sake of the mission of the church, but also because of its contribution to the way in which we understand the world and the insight which it offers into the human situation. Anyone who claims to have a religious faith needs to be able to relate that faith to all of the events which occur around them, including those which are troublesome and shocking. Faith has to interact with the whole of our human experience. An understanding of both science and theology, together with their interaction and relationship, is therefore essential if a religious person is to be able to make a meaningful response to natural disasters such as tsunamis, drought, earthquakes and hurricanes. Indeed, such a response is likely to become increasingly important in the coming years as the phenomenon of climate change, caused by anthropogenic emissions of greenhouse gases, is liable to make droughts, hurricanes and other extreme weather patterns increasingly common.

When science and theology are discussed together in the present day, the issues for discussion usually concern various aspects of modern physics such as cosmology, subatomic particles, quantum mechanics and theories of relativity. Writers frequently concentrate on showing how there is no necessary conflict between the two disciplines and that both are capable of describing the world as it actually is. There is a similar continuing interest in the relationship between theology and evolution. These debates concerning the relationship of theology with physics and with biology overlap in their discussion on the origins of the universe and of life. However, much less attention has been paid to the involvement of the third traditional scientific discipline in this debate and as a result the relationship between chemistry and theology has largely been neglected. This has occurred despite the work of the eminent theoretical chemist, Charles Coulson, whose writings during the 1950s prefigured the later work of British authors such as Arthur Peacocke and John Polkinghorne. This omission of chemistry from the science and theology dialogue is not surprising, since it seems to involve neither the fundamentals of the universe nor the origins of life. At first sight the interaction between chemistry and theology would appear to have little potential for major conflict, as well as little opportunity to illustrate the parallels which may exist between the two fields of study.

However, there is at least one important aspect of chemistry which may offer profound parallels with Christian theological discourse and which lies at the very heart of chemical processes. It is an aspect which is involved in physical descriptions of the way in which the universe behaves and biological descriptions of life and death, as well as being related to the occurrence of natural disasters. It is also an aspect where theology can respond with its own parallel and enter a genuine dialogue, rather than having to respond to the way in which science impinges upon its beliefs. This fundamental aspect of our scientific understanding of the universe is the Second Law of Thermodynamics.

The Second Law of Thermodynamics is familiar to all students of physical science and those branches of engineering which involve heat-transfer. It is a law which is expressed in many forms, the simplest of which is the apparently obvious statement:

Heat cannot flow spontaneously from a colder to a hotter body. An example of this is the fact that at normal room temperatures an ice cube will melt but a pool of water will not spontaneously form itself into ice. This is a law which lies behind a large number of everyday processes, from refrigeration to the internal combustion engine, as well as having implications for living creatures. It is therefore unfortunate that, unlike its more fashionable counterparts in modern physics, it is not a household name, nor has it been invoked to any great extent in the discussion which is increasingly occurring between science and theology.

In some ways this book is an attempt to remedy this omission. It does so in part by exploring the parallels which may exist between the Second Law of Thermodynamics and the Christian doctrine of Original Sin. In the process it therefore, by implication, says something about natural disasters and human evil. It addresses the questions as to why we suffer through disease and human violence and why God allows natural forces such as tsunamis, earthquakes, volcanic eruptions, hurricanes and floods to cause harm. The book also provides an introduction to the relationship between science and religion, as well as considering the wider relationship between the Second Law of Thermodynamics and Christian faith, doctrine and practice. However, it is important to realize that this exploration is not carried out in an attempt to provide a synthesis of the two fields of study, nor is it done in an attempt to provide a scientific proof for Original Sin or a theological justification for science.

This is not a book of Christian apologetics which has been written in order to justify the Christian faith in a scientific age – if it does find a place in such apologetics then this is a bonus rather than an intention. If science and theology are of any value at all then they both have to describe the world as it actually is and they must both concern themselves with the totality of experience and everything there is, rather than making philosophical claims which bear no apparent relationship to everyday life. If they can both describe the world in this way then we should not be surprised if we find a number of parallels between them. The virtue and interest of such parallels lies in the questions which the two disciplines may ask of each other and in the answers which we can provide to those questions.

In the discussion of the Second Law and its consequences I have deliberately avoided the use of mathematical equations wherever possible, knowing that they would provide a stumbling block to many readers who do not have a scientific or mathematical background. I apologize for this decision to those readers who are scientists or who might have welcomed such equations. Those who welcome their omission might also like to reflect on how those who write and speak from inside the Christian faith can sometimes provide stumbling blocks for those on the outside through their similar use of jargon or specialist language.

In similar vein, I have also felt it necessary to review certain elements of Christian theology, such as the theories put forward to explain the atonement – that branch of theology which explains what Jesus achieved on the cross. However, in doing this I have tried to avoid a textbook approach but instead to be constructively critical of these theories using the framework of the present discussion as a basis for the criticism. As a result, rather than merely reviewing the content of these ideas, we can discover which of them have the power to address the issues under discussion and provide answers to the questions which are being asked in the present day.

I also hope that the present discussion will have implications for Christian faith and life and that some of its conclusions will relate to and inform pastoral practice. If theology is to be of any value, then it needs to inform our faith in God as well as our more academic thoughts about the divine. This is the traditional English way of a speculative-affective synthesis in spirituality; the interpenetration of the mind and the feelings of devotion.

Indeed, I hope that these ideas may be fruitful in providing the starting point for developments and details which have been precluded within the present study.

If there is one sense in which the contents of this book cause me to hesitate, it would be the potential misunderstanding that I am trying to produce a synthesis of theology and science, or to integrate the two disciplines in some grandiose scheme which subverts the truths of both of them. This is not the case. In my scientific research, the approach I followed was always quite orthodox and I describe my Christian beliefs as traditional. This book is intended as a dialogue between two disciplines which are both, hopefully, describing the universe as it actually is.

I am grateful to Peter Selby, the then Bishop of Worcester, and to the late Brother Bernard SSF who both stressed to me that I should leave my parishes to fend for themselves for one day each month to create the space which would allow me to go away to a quiet place in order to study and to write. I am also grateful to Kate Bird, who read through an early draft of the manuscript and made a number of suggestions for improvement and change in emphasis. David Walker, Bishop of Dudley, read a later version of the whole manuscript and made a number of helpful suggestions for expansion and restructuring, one of which led to the discovery of further insights and parallels. Sophie Hunt proofread the final manuscript and made a number of corrections to my punctuation and spelling. My final thanks go to Michael Langrish, Bishop of Exeter, who encouraged me to undertake the final rewrite and who has kindly contributed the foreword.

Adrian Hough
Exeter
Trinity Sunday 2009

1

Introduction

We begin with two quotations

> The small child who tosses a toy or a blanket or some other imperfectly elastic object from his crib soon learns what to expect. The tossed object will fall to the floor, and there it will come to rest, eventually. The process is entirely spontaneous and completely irreversible. Never does the object at some later time come back spontaneously to the crib. In common with other spontaneous processes, the process results in a net increase in the disorder of the universe.[1]

> So when the woman saw that the tree was good for food, and that it was a delight to the eyes, and that the tree was to be desired to make one wise, she took of its fruit and ate; and she also gave some to her husband, who was with her, and he ate. Then the eyes of both were opened, and they knew that they were naked; and they sewed fig leaves together and made loincloths for themselves ...
>
> Then the LORD God said, 'See, the man has become like one of us, knowing good and evil; and now, he might reach out his hand and take from the tree of life, and eat, and live for ever'.[2]

In 1922 the French paleontologist and Jesuit priest, Pierre Teilhard de Chardin, was invited to write a paper indicating three different ways in which the doctrine of Original Sin might be presented to people who were not convinced by the official formulations of the Roman Catholic Church. His response to this request was never published because a draft of the paper was apparently stolen from his desk and sent to the Church authorities in Rome. The consequence of this draft being read by those of a conservative doctrinal disposition was that Teilhard de Chardin was effectively forbidden from saying or writing anything on this subject which deviated from the official Church formulations. Indeed, the consequences were to restrict his freedom of speech and movement for the rest of his life. [3]

We do not know the content of this draft paper, but Robert Speaight reports that a study of Teilhard de Chardin's correspondence indicates that amongst the ideas which he had propounded was the suggestion that Original Sin might be a necessary flaw in the universe. Such a suggestion that the divine creation could be faulty in itself – rather than Sin being introduced through human disobedience – would clearly have been anathema to the authorities in Rome and would in itself be sufficient to explain their action taken against the author. The same reaction would have been made to his later statement that the idea of sin would one day be assimilated into the idea of progress because such progress is inevitably accompanied by sin.[4]

It is unfortunate that Teilhard de Chardin was never allowed to develop these ideas concerning Original Sin further, at least not in any form which has survived in print, for they contained the seeds of a very fruitful dialogue between science and Christian theology. In many ways they can be seen as an undeveloped foretaste to the present work which might also seem to suggest that Original Sin is 'necessary' and that 'Sin' always and inevitably accompanies any change which occurs and is therefore a bedfellow of progress. However, in drawing such a conclusion at this point in the discussion, a great deal of detail would have been lost and the precise meaning of the terminology in this particular context would have been ignored. In the same way, we shall never know the arguments which would have been contained in the final version of Teilhard de Chardin's paper and the caveats which he might have placed upon the language which he used. Indeed, in the intervening years, the whole concept of Original Sin has become somewhat unfashionable, partly due to the cult of human progress of which Teilhard de Chardin was himself an exponent and partly because of the distaste with which it is often viewed by those who have read only simplistic explanations or caricatures of this important Christian doctrine.

In his book *The Stranger in the Wings*, Richard Holloway, the former Primus of the Scottish Episcopal Church, expresses an opinion which runs contrary to the above fashion when he notes that Original Sin is the most empirical of the Christian doctrines.[5] He bases this claim on his observation that human nature contains a bias or tendency which distorts and vitiates all our relationships and institutions. He writes that Original Sin is the theological equivalent of 'Murphy's Law', that semi-serious expression of popular philosophy, which states that if a thing can go wrong then it will. The derivation of theological or scientific ideas from commonplace truths in this way is what writers such as John Polkinghorne have termed 'bottom-up-thinking'.[6]

Murphy's Law summarizes the wry observation that the world has a tendency to go wrong and that it has an inherent disorder built into it. Things in the world have a tendency to fall apart, and having fallen apart it is unheard of for them to fall back together again. Material objects wear out, houses need cleaning and weeds grow in what was once a neat and tidy garden. Holloway's comparison of Murphy's Law with Original Sin is quite apt because they both point to the fact that the world and human relationships fail to live up to the ideal which we might wish was the case. When we compare what we observe in the world with a hypothetical ideal then it does indeed appear as if there is a flaw in the universe. However, although Murphy's Law is a popular observation of the world, it also bears a certain amount of scientific scrutiny, for it appears to be very similar to the Second Law of Thermodynamics. This fundamental scientific principle can be expressed in many different ways, but one of them is a statement that the disorder of the universe is continually increasing; that things have a tendency to break down and to go wrong.

Human nature contains a tendency which distorts our relationships; things have a tendency to go wrong; and the disorder of the universe always increases with the passage of time. These are three similar statements; one of them derives from Christian theology, one from popular observation and one from scientific study. Is their similarity merely a coincidence or is there a more profound parallel between them? Is it possible that Original Sin and the Second Law of Thermodynamics correspond to each other in some way and that Murphy's Law, a wry and cynical observation of the world, is actually a popular outworking of these two ideas? Are Original Sin and the Second Law of Thermodynamics the ways in which two somewhat different disciplines express the same fundamental truth and is it possible that they could both contribute to our theological understanding of natural disasters as well as human evil? Are they manifestations of what Teilhard de Chardin described as a fundamental 'flaw in the universe' – a flaw which causes both natural disasters, such as a tsunami or an earthquake, as well as those which occur due to the interaction of human actions and natural events such as the landslide which occurred at the Welsh village of Aberfan in the 1960s, killing all the pupils and staff at the local school.

If the answer to these questions is in any way 'yes', then this is an observation of profound importance and significance, not least because of the mutual illumination which these statements might provide. It might be that scientific and theological descriptions of the world are closer to each other than is often thought to be the case. This possible parallel between the doctrine of

Original Sin and the Second Law of Thermodynamics will form the basis for many of the issues which we shall be exploring throughout this book, including those of human suffering, illness and natural disaster.

1.1 Sin, Disaster, Death and Salvation

The Christian faith is centered around the belief that people are saved through the death and resurrection of Jesus Christ, the Son of God. 'Jesus Saves' is a slogan found on the outside of many church buildings. There is a clear belief that we are saved, but this statement of belief begs the question as to the nature of that from which salvation occurs. Different Christian groups express this in different ways and a cynic might argue that there is little evidence of our being saved from death, disaster and human malevolence and therefore want to challenge this whole claim.

The usual response to the question is that we are saved from the consequences of our sins or from our Sin. Although these two words ('sins' and 'Sin') appear to be quite similar and are often used interchangeably, it is important to note that they can carry an important and significant distinction. Our sins can be thought of as our moral misdeeds, what is sometimes described as 'moral evil', in order to distinguish it from natural disasters or genuine accidents for which no-one is to blame and which come under the description of 'physical evil'. If we are saved from our sins or misdeeds, then we are presumably saved from the punishment which we deserve for committing these misdeeds.

In distinction to sins, Sin itself (in the singular and a proper noun) can be considered as a basic human state or condition which disrupts the relationships of which we are a part and which therefore results in the possibility of our committing sins or moral misdeeds in the first place. It is what John Polkinghorne has described as 'a dark side to human nature, that inherent flaw by which our better aspirations are frustrated'. [7] This is the same state which is often described by the term 'Original Sin'. In this

12

case, if we are saved, then we are saved from a fundamental problem with human nature rather than from punishment for our moral misdeeds. In this sense, at least, we are saved from the consequences of a flaw in the universe. This distinction between sins and Sin is important in the discussions to come. Throughout this book the word 'sins' (lower case and plural) will be used to refer to moral misdeeds, whereas the word 'Sin' (upper case and singular) will be used to refer to flawed human nature or Original Sin.

However, there is also a further answer to the question of our salvation, and that is that despite the query of the cynic, we are indeed all saved from death through the claim that death is not final and that we can experience a new life beyond our worldly grave. In chapter 3 of John's Gospel, Jesus tells Nicodemus, who has come to question Him, that 'God so loved the world that he gave his only Son, so that everyone who believes in him may not perish but may have eternal life'. Human death is a particular example of the fact that all creatures die and that natural disasters occur in the world – a state of affairs which could be described as a flaw. This combination of death and natural disaster falls into the category of 'physical evil' and is seen as an inevitable consequence of a world which is exploring and realizing its own potentiality.[8] Salvation is therefore not just an issue of sins or Sin, it is also a matter of life and death – a second sense in which we are saved from a flaw in the universe. Indeed, since it is contended that Sin (as opposed to sins) is not about moral decisions but actually concerns the fundamental human condition, it too should count as 'physical evil' rather than 'moral evil'.

Now these two themes of Sin and death are related in that they can be understood as opposite sides of the same theological coin. St Paul made this connection, claiming that death is the result of Sin. In chapter 5 of his letter to the Romans, St Paul set out one possible version of his understanding of this subject. He wrote that death came into the world through Sin and that Sin came into the world through the disobedience of Adam in the Garden of Eden. St Paul's explanation of salvation was apparently based on the understanding that just as Sin entered into the human race through the disobedience of Adam, in his eating from the tree of the knowledge of good and evil, so salvation comes to the human race through the obedience of one man who died on the cross. Jesus died for our sins, or moral misdeeds, and in His overcoming death He also overcame the fundamental condition which theologians have called 'Sin'. Whether we understand chapter 3 of the biblical book of Genesis in literal or in mythical terms, its role in Christian doctrine has been to state the presence of Sin in the world (i.e. the propensity and inevitability of human disobedience and immorality) and to provide an account of human mortality. Once Adam and Eve had been expelled from the garden because of their disobedience, they had no opportunity to eat from the tree of life and they and their descendants were therefore condemned to die.

James Barr has argued that the loss of immortality is really the whole point of this narrative from the opening chapters of Genesis. Rather than being concerned with the origins of Original Sin, the account of Adam and Eve was originally provided to account for human mortality and why human beings necessarily have to die. In this scheme of things, Adam and Eve, acting on our behalf, chose knowledge and mortality rather than ignorance and everlasting life. As the narrative proceeds through the early chapters of Genesis, the lifespan of the characters decreases as their mortality becomes increasingly apparent. Barr makes the point that there is no mention of Sin in the third chapter of Genesis.[9] Barr also makes the observation that Paul's argument concerning Adam and Sin, in that Jesus died for all in the same way as Adam sinned for all, is in biblical terms uniquely Pauline. It occurs nowhere else in the New Testament. He claims that Paul is using a typology to make a point rather than developing a major piece of doctrine. The reference to Sin has been overemphasized ever since and the original meaning of the Genesis narrative, which was an explanation of human mortality, has thereby been lost. Indeed, the fundamental underlying truth of Original Sin was brought into disrepute because of the conclusions which could be drawn from Paul's typology. Patristic writings in which Original Sin was seen as being inherited from Adam were later used to discredit the whole doctrine because they appeared to remove individual responsibility for sinful actions. Pannenberg makes the point that it was Paul's observation of universal death which led him to deduce the universal presence of Sin as a fundamental human condition.[10] In struggling to explain why we are condemned to die, Paul concluded that this apparent flaw in the universe, the final enemy which must be overcome, must be present due to a human misdeed.

In his argument, Barr is keen to emphasize that he is not arguing against the existence of Original Sin. Like Holloway, he makes it quite clear that he regards its existence as an obvious conclusion to draw from looking at the world. Any serious observation of human behavior makes it quite clear that human nature is flawed, irrespective of what idealists might tell us. At the very least, the doctrine of Original Sin is a good corrective to a naive optimism and is based firmly on observation.

This same conclusion was reached by Paul Tillich, who noted that not only humanity but the whole universe is estranged from its ideal nature, an estrangement which Tillich called the 'fall from essence to existence'.[11] In individual terms, Sin expresses the inbuilt and unconscious turning away from the ideal self with its allegiance to God as the center of life (an allegiance which Tillich called 'belief') and the placing of the self at the center of attention. Once it is at the center, then the self attempts to take hold of all power and control.[12] In simple terms, human beings are inherently self-centered and want their own way. In theological terms they have failed to accept their creaturely status and their subservience to God. We should note that this link between love of the self and a turning away from God was noted in the early fifth century by Augustine, who saw it as a universal human flaw. However, the discrediting of other Augustinian ideas, such as the concept of inherited Sin and the associated inherited guilt, which began in the sixteenth century, prevented Christianity from holding on to this important truth.[13] It was only when such inherited guilt had been discredited that the structural universality of Sin, and what this implied about the human condition, could be considered seriously.

Tillich went on to argue that Sin is not like the laws of nature, but is rather a matter of personal freedom and universal destiny. By personal freedom he seems to have meant that Sin involves an individual turning away from God and towards the self – he does not appear to have been suggesting that we have the ability not to commit moral misdemeanors. However, if Sin is a matter of universal destiny, as Tillich suggests, then although this reinforces the view that we cannot avoid such Sin, it also suggests that it operates as a general principle. If Sin appears as a universal and general principle throughout the universe, then surely this does place it on a par with the laws of nature. Viewed from the perspective of someone who does not want to die, this state of affairs is a serious flaw.

The earlier statement that Sin and death are opposite sides of the same coin is a useful claim. The Christian church has, quite rightly, long emphasized salvation from our sins or moral misdemeanors, but it has not been so up-front in its claims concerning salvation from the consequences of suffering and of death. Yet it seems to be a matter of simple observation that, in the present day, death and suffering are usually somewhat higher on people's personal and communal list of real concerns than are the moral misdeeds which are reported in the press on a daily basis. This is particularly the case when death occurs prematurely, whether this is through disease, disaster, accident or human ill-will. The fact that there is very little interest in the answers which the church may be able to provide to these problems of human existence suggests that any previous answers have been seen as irrelevant or unhelpful.

A change of emphasis in the response in order to deal with suffering and untimely death could well address people's needs and feelings more adequately than would a continuing preoccupation with Sin. This is not to claim that it is right or wrong for people to have this priority in their lives, but simply to observe that if they do have this priority then the Christian resource which answers their questions is that of eternal life rather than salvation from sins. As an example, when a tsunami devastated much of the coastline of the Indian Ocean on 26th December in 2004, how many of those who had to preach a sermon on the following Sunday provided anything near to a coherent explanation of how this could be reconciled with belief in a God of Love in the words which they used within their sermons?

The subject of death is one which is all too often glossed over with the message that it is merely a minor point along the road to something better which God will provide for those who love Him. Yet this pious platitude simply will not do. Not only is it insulting to those who have to watch their loved ones die, but it also flies in the face of the evidence which we find in the life of Jesus Himself. Confronted with the death of His friend Lazarus, Jesus wept. He did not tell Lazarus' sisters, Martha and Mary, that all was well because Lazarus was now with his Father and that he would rise again on the last day; instead Jesus wept. He wept at the fate of Lazarus because a friend was dead and He wept at the fate of each one of us and He wept because He knew what He must experience for Himself.

The statement that each member of the human race will one day have to die is generally accepted as a matter of fact. Such a universal destiny demands a universal explanation. In terms of the traditional Christian theological story the explanation for this condition is provided by Original Sin. This Original Sin consists in a universal flaw or 'fallenness' in human nature which manifests itself both in the fact that we all commit moral misdeeds and in the death of each human individual. Indeed, this 'flaw' appears to extend to the whole of the creation, not least because of the effects of what we usually term 'natural' disasters. This universal flaw in the universe is what Tom Wright has termed 'a cosmic dislocation between the creator and the creation'[14] and what John Polkinghorne has termed 'physical evil'. Death is an essential consequence of Sin. The only hope lies in God's forgiveness and in His annulment of Sin itself; His bringing the world to the end for which it was intended. In Christian terms this is the only route which can lead to eternal life.

1.2 The Second Law of Thermodynamics

The First Law of Thermodynamics is sometimes known as the Law of the Conservation of Energy and states that energy can neither be created nor destroyed.[15] This means that in all physical or chemical processes there is no overall change in the total amount of energy involved. When we burn a log on the fire, chemical energy is turned into heat energy and when we drop a book, gravitational energy is again turned into heat. When a car accelerates, the chemical energy in its fuel is transformed into the kinetic energy of the moving car together with the heat which is produced both in the engine and through friction with the surface of the road.

The Second Law of Thermodynamics is more involved than the First Law and lies behind a great many everyday phenomena which we usually take for granted. In our earlier example, when we burned the log, we produced heat, ash, smoke and a number of invisible gases such as carbon dioxide. We would not expect to see all these products spontaneously reforming themselves into the log. Similarly, we do not expect a book to suddenly jump off the floor and place itself in our hand nor a car to slow down and regenerate the petrol which it used to accelerate in the first place. Children's toys, scattered on the floor, do not magically put themselves away. The conclusion to draw from this everyday common sense is that although energy is always conserved in a physical or chemical process, it does not follow that these processes can be reversed. If we film a bouncing ball gradually bouncing lower and lower until it stops, we know that the film will look unreal and absurd if it is played in reverse. That is why children can derive so much pleasure from such a film. They instinctively know that what is being shown runs contrary to the nature of the world around them, even though they cannot give a scientific explanation as to why it is nonsense.

Each of the above examples illustrates the way in which a spontaneous process will proceed in one direction but not in the reverse. The Second Law of Thermodynamics describes the direction in which the spontaneous process will proceed, although the way in which this law is expressed varies from author to author. We have already seen one statement of the law, namely: *Heat cannot flow spontaneously from a colder to a hotter body.* Two other more general statements express the sense of direction which is present in a spontaneous change and the underlying principle which is involved.

One version relevant to chemical thermodynamics states: *Spontaneous changes are those which, if carried out under the proper conditions, can be made to do work. If carried out reversibly they yield a maximum amount of work. In natural processes the maximum work is never obtained.*[16] (The term 'work' is generally defined as the useful application of heat or other energy released during the process in question – perhaps to generate electricity or to propel a car.) The conclusion to note from this form of the law is that natural spontaneous processes are generally non-reversible and that the maximum amount of work cannot be obtained from them. Some of the work which could potentially have been obtained (for example, to generate electricity or to move a car) has been lost along the way.

Another formulation of the law is: *In isolated systems undergoing natural irreversible processes, the entropy and 'disorder' (appropriately defined) always increase.*[17] Here we have the underlying feature of the Second Law, namely that the irreversibility is due to the increase in disorder (or entropy) which accompanies a natural spontaneous process. This increase in disorder is a measure of the potential work which was available (for example, to generate electricity or to propel a car) but which has been lost along the way. As it happens, states of a higher disorder are more probable than those of a lower disorder[18] and so, as we might instinctively expect, a natural spontaneous process moves from a less probable state to a more probable state. A trivial example of this movement is that if we drop a packet of sugar onto the floor then the granules will tend to spread out all over the floor rather than to conveniently arrange themselves in a neat and regularly packed cube. Indeed, the chance of them forming such a cube is so unlikely that we would never expect to observe it even if we were to spend our entire life pouring bags of sugar onto the floor.

Whenever a natural spontaneous process occurs, it is always accompanied by an increase in the total disorder or entropy. When a book falls off a shelf and lands on the floor, this greater disorder appears in the increased motion of the molecules which make up the book, the floor and the air through which the book fell. This greater disorder is more likely than the more ordered state which existed before the book fell from the shelf. The reverse process, namely that of the book leaping off the floor and onto the shelf, being propelled in the process by a sudden ordered motion of the molecules in the floor, is beyond our experience because such a motion is highly improbable. Such a leap by the book would involve a significant increase in the ordering of the universe, as the molecules of the floor and the book all suddenly vibrated in the necessary synchronized way.

The measurable amount of disorder possessed by a physical object is described as its entropy. For a given substance under given conditions, such as a fixed temperature, the entropy is always the same.[19] In general, gases have a greater entropy or disorder than liquids which, in turn, have a greater entropy than solids. In a solid the atoms or molecules can only vibrate about a fixed position. In a liquid they are free to rotate and move at random with respect to each other. In a gas this rotation and motion is much less hindered because the atoms or molecules are much further apart. Substances tend to be solids at lower temperatures and gases at higher temperatures because the greater disorder becomes more significant at higher temperatures.

It is important to realize that the increase in entropy which accompanies a spontaneous process is always an increase as measured for the system as a whole. Unless we have constructed a specially isolated system, such as we might wish to do in a laboratory experiment, then this system is generally taken to be the whole universe and we assume that the universe behaves as an isolated or closed system. However, since it is only the entropy of the whole system or universe which has to increase, it is possible for isolated local pockets of order to exist, in which the entropy decreases, although this will always be at the expense of a corresponding increase elsewhere. This is what allows animals to construct structures which contain order. Indeed, this is what allows living organisms to exist at all, since a living organism is a local pocket of order in which food and oxygen are used to produce ordered living tissue. As Arthur Peacocke has discussed, organization and complexity are only produced in systems which are open, non-linear and far from equilibrium.[20] In other words, organization and complexity can occur only in systems which can get rid of molecular disorder to somewhere else, and the resulting system is intrinsically unstable. If such a system is left unattended with no input of energy, then it will decay – a simple example being that if animals do not eat then they will starve to death. The tendency towards increasing complexity which is present within nature, and which appears to run contrary to the Second Law of Thermodynamics, occurs because living organisms are open systems which use energy to export entropy or disorder to their surroundings. Indeed, at low temperatures, it is possible for the production of large molecules of great complexity to be driven by the greater degree of randomization and therefore entropy which is possible in such molecules.[21]

The death of a living organism occurs due to the breakdown of its biological organization and the eventual dispersal of its atoms and molecules. This can occur suddenly through some trauma, more slowly as a disease destroys the internal organization of the body, or very slowly due to the processes of ageing.[22] Ageing involves the build-up of random errors in a body's genetic material, with the disorder consisting of the increasing randomness which is present in these codes. Disorder here occurs in the genetic codes which describe the way in which the body is constructed. Beyond a certain point, the number of errors which are present become incompatible with the continuation of life. To reverse this building-up of errors indefinitely would be to break the Second Law. Ultimately, it is the Second Law of Thermodynamics which kills every living creature. If we wish to remain fit, healthy and active for ever, then the Second Law of Thermodynamics constitutes a fundamental flaw in the universe.

1.3 The Second Law and Sin

According to the New Testament, Sin (understood again as Sin itself rather than moral misdeeds) results in death. According to physical science, the Second Law of Thermodynamics leads to the breakdown of individual organisms and their death. In both cases, and in terms of their own discipline, these are seen as fundamental rules which describe the way in which the universe exists and operates. If we were to use the language of Teilhard de Chardin, then we might say that all progress involves change and that, following the principles of the Second Law of Thermodynamics, progress therefore has to involve an increase in the disorder of the universe. Since this disorder produces decay and death then, from the perspective of living creatures, it can be seen as a flaw or imperfection. The theological questions are whether this continuous increase in the disorder of the creation actually has to be the case and whether this apparent flaw really is a flaw and whether it was and is necessary.

Before we can begin to answer these questions, as well as addressing the issue as to whether the doctrine of Original Sin and the Second Law of Thermodynamics are opposite sides of the same coin, a coin which we might want to call 'death', we will need to explore them both in more detail. In so doing, it will be necessary for us to gain an understanding of the relationship which exists between science and theology so that this possible parallel can be placed in the appropriate context and examined from a similar perspective. It will also be necessary to examine both the Second Law of Thermodynamics and the issues relating to Sin itself in more detail. Because the atonement – the effect which Jesus' death on the cross has upon us and upon the universe – forms the divine response and solution to Sin, it will then be important for this to be included in our considerations. If parallels do exist between the Second Law and Original Sin, as we shall claim that they do, then the Christian account of how Sin and death are overcome not only needs to be part of the story which we consider, but it also has questions to ask of the Second Law of Thermodynamics as well as becoming part of our response to physical evil such as natural disasters. These are the issues which we shall examine in the next three chapters, before we move on to look at some of the other consequences which result from this thinking. It will also be important for us to consider the implications of the Second Law of Thermodynamics and its relationship with Sin for other aspects of Christian doctrine, such as the Trinity, Christology, theodicy and the Eucharist. If these relationships can be mutually informative, then this will have something to say to our wider Christian beliefs, not least to the resurrection of Jesus which, at first sight, would appear to be a violation of the Second Law. In each case, the relationship between Sin and the doctrine under consideration has already been the subject of a great deal of theological discussion and is not of particular interest to us here. Our main concern will be in whether the Second Law of Thermodynamics can also be a part of the discussion – both with and without considering the notion of Original Sin. If it can, then this should not be seen as a threat to Christian faith and belief, but should rather lead us into a deeper understanding of theology and an increasing robustness to our faith.

However, it is important to realize that these are not simply dry issues for theological debate and discussion. These are questions which affect every single person every day of their life. They are issues which concern the practicalities of life and death. They are the answers to natural disasters, to fatal illness and to blatant human cruelty, as well as to the questions which ask how a loving and powerful God can allow such things to happen. In short, these are questions both of everyday life and of the practical outworkings of the Christian faith. The arguments and the responses which we develop as a response to the human question are of vital importance to the way in which the Christian church acts within the world and speaks to it in its times of crisis. The blunt truth is that Christian theology has never provided a truly satisfactory answer to the question of human suffering other than those which will satisfy people who are already firmly convinced of the claims made by the Christian faith.

However, before we can begin to explore these issues, and especially before the relationship between science and theology can be placed under scrutiny, it is necessary to pay attention to the standpoint from which we shall examine these issues. In any discussions such as these we always approach the issue influenced by our own prior knowledge and feelings. There is no such thing as a truly objective discussion. In this case our knowledge of and our attitude towards both science and Christianity will influence the outcome and introduce an inevitable bias in the results.[23] Indeed, unless we are to argue that science and Christian theology can be completely integrated (see section 2.2), then we must stand in one camp or the other, even though we may attempt to spend some time in each of them. As someone who has trained in both science and Christian theology and who has worked both as a scientist and as a parish priest and who has also taught some theology, I have stood in both camps and in this book I will attempt to do so again. However, I am writing primarily from the perspective of a Christian theologian, not as a scientist, and I am writing primarily for people who have an interest in the Christian faith (which, of course, includes many scientists) rather than for scientists themselves. What I write is therefore colored by the worldview of Christian theology even if I attempt to avoid such a perspective or bias. This worldview determines my standpoint and it must therefore be explored.

In his book *The New Testament and the People of God*, Tom Wright examines the worldview which he believes underlies Christian theology, together with some of the consequences of this worldview.[24] His account provides a useful backdrop to the present discussions because his theological presuppositions appear to be similar to those which lie behind the present study. According to Wright there are four points which characterize the Christian worldview and which therefore underlie Christian theology. The first of these is that it tells a coherent story, the second that it provides answers to the four questions of existence which must be answered by any worldview, the third that it finds expression in symbolic artefacts and events, and the fourth that it gives rise to a particular way of living in the world.

If we consider first the coherent story which the Christian worldview tells, then according to Wright:

> The story is about a creator and his creation, about humans made in this creator's image and given tasks to perform, about the rebellion of humans and the dissonance of creation at every level, and particularly about the creator's acting, through Israel and climactically through Jesus, to rescue his creation from its ensuing plight. The story continues with the creator acting by his own spirit within the world to bring it towards the restoration which his intended goal for it.[25]

This is the story of creation, Original Sin, the atonement and God's gift of the Holy Spirit. It is a story which provides a good starting point if we are to discuss the nature of matter, the relationship between Original Sin and the Second Law, and what the implications of this relationship might be for the doctrine of the atonement. In this sense at least, Wright's Christian worldview coincides with the issues which we need to address.

The four questions of existence which Wright believes must be answered by any worldview begin with the question 'Who are we?' The answer he gives is that we are humans made in the image of the creator. The second question he asks is 'Where are we?' and he finds the answer that we are in a good and beautiful, though transient, world. In the context of the present book, we should note that in scientific terms this world has to be transient because of the Second Law of Thermodynamics and that from the human perspective, although the world may well be beautiful, the world is also very flawed. Thirdly he asks 'What is wrong?' and discovers that humanity has rebelled against the creator. Wright adds that this rebellion reflects a cosmic dislocation between the creator and the creation and in this sense we can understand it as but one manifestation of a far greater truth. We should also note that this dislocation or flaw looks something like the Second Law of Thermodynamics. If we wanted to use less theological language we might say that human behavior runs contrary to the nature of the universe. His fourth question, namely 'What is the solution?' is answered by the creator acting within His creation to deal with the human rebellion and to bring the world to the end for which it was made. If the parallels which we are exploring prove to be fruitful then we will have to consider what consequences this may have for the Second Law of Thermodynamics. We should also note that Wright believes, quite rightly, that many branches of Christianity have not adopted this four-point ground plan and that they have therefore twisted the Christian faith into a new design which is made in their own image.

Moving on to the third of the points which Wright uses to describe the Christian worldview, namely that of symbols and artefacts, we should observe that the symbolic artefacts and cultural events which characterize Christianity include both church architecture and the liturgy of Christian worship, and that this includes both the Eucharist and prayer. Particularly where such artefacts and events acquire symbolic value, they can help people to make sense of their lives and to live those lives coherently. However, it is the cross which is the symbol which sums up the Christian faith beyond all other symbols and which has given hope and inspiration to countless people throughout the centuries. The cross has come to play this central role because it is crucial to the story and because it is involved with the death, life and salvation which occurs in Jesus Christ. Any such symbol or artefact which marks the conquest of death and Sin clearly needs to be a part of our discussions, but it is the cross which is the most important. The crucifixion of Jesus and the value of the cross in the present day are both crucial issues for us to consider. There is a very real sense in which the whole of the argument hangs upon the cross.

Finally, there is the issue of Christian praxis, the way of 'being a Christian' in the world. Although this includes elements of prayer and the life of the church, it also encompasses life in a much wider sense. It has to do with the whole of our existence, as well as the way in which we cope with both physical and moral evil and with the prospect of our own end. We could say that it is here that we find the outworking of the Christian response to the Second Law: a law which affects us at every moment of our lives but which most of the time goes unnoticed. Such a law, which lies behind the description of most events of everyday life, is clearly of fundamental importance. Its interaction with the Christian gospel is one of the questions for which theology needs an answer if it is to relate in a meaningful way to the world in which we live, and yet it is a relationship which has been persistently ignored. In general terms, it is this interaction between the Second Law of Thermodynamics and the Christian gospel and the consequences of this interaction which form the subject matter of this book.

The Relationship between Science and Theology

This book is concerned with the relationship between the Second Law of Thermodynamics and Christian doctrine. It explores, in particular, the parallels which may exist between the Second Law of Thermodynamics and the Doctrine of Original Sin and the ways in which this relationship can inform our theology of physical and moral evil – what can the relationship teach us about human suffering and natural disaster? However, before we can investigate a subject which draws on the results and content of religious belief and theology on the one hand, and science on the other, we need first to establish the ground rules. We need to be clear about our understanding of the relationship which exists between these subjects. We shall therefore begin this chapter with a brief historical perspective before moving on to consider the relationship which exists between religious beliefs and science. This will also involve an examination of the possible similarities in theological and scientific methods before we finally consider the ways in which these subjects all influence our view of the world.

2.1 An Historical Perspective

One of the widely held and popular opinions of the present day is that religious belief is incompatible with the methodology and results of modern science.[1] Arthur Peacocke has summarized this situation as follows.

The understanding of the world which is evoked by the contemporary natural sciences is commonly taken in the West to be inimical to, or at least subversive of, religious belief in general and Christian belief in particular.[2]

Two or more centuries ago, such a view would have been unthinkable. Scientists such as Isaac Newton believed that the study of nature was a religious duty, because to study nature was also to study the divine order,[3] and many scientists of the seventeenth and earlier centuries were themselves clergymen. Even in the mid-nineteenth century, Charles Darwin could consider that his studies enhanced the view of God rather than being an argument against God's providence, and it is an often ignored fact that his critic, Bishop Samuel Wilberforce, was a vice-president of the British Association.[4] Nowadays, it is more common to hear the opposite view, with debate on both radio and television focusing attention on what the participants in such debates often see as irreconcilable differences between scientific study and the tenets of Christian belief. It is claimed that theologians are guilty of ignoring the results of scientific investigation and that they are out of touch with the reality of the universe.

However, this opinion is by no means universal. Over sixty years ago, the Cambridge theologian Charles Raven attacked the damage which had been done by the 'over-rigid differentiation between science and other subjects of enquiry and research'.[5] Raven also attacked the widely held notion that anyone is capable of writing a book on theology, a task which is sometimes undertaken in order to refute various theological claims. He noted that in contrast to the situation with theology, when writing a book in most other subjects, some indication of competence and training in the area of study would be required before the opinions of the author would be taken seriously, although this is now far less true than it was when Raven made his claim. It is now over fifty years since the Oxford theoretical chemist, Charles Coulson, delivered the John Calvin McNair Lectures at the University of Chapel Hill, North Carolina in which he addressed the relationship between science and Christian belief. The general principles of the relationship between science and Christian belief as outlined by Charles Coulson in the 1950s are still as relevant today as they were then.[6]

In more recent times, the claim that religious belief is incompatible with science has repeatedly been challenged by authors such as John Polkinghorne, Arthur Peacocke and Russell Stannard, all of whom gained their reputation as scientists prior to their studying and writing about theology and its relationship with science. This debate has since been joined by Alister McGrath, another theologian who began as a scientist. There are a great many scientists who are active members of the Christian church and a significant number of ordained members of the churches who began their higher education by studying science at university. We should also note that science itself is nowadays frequently viewed with suspicion by many people, albeit that they continue to enjoy its benefits, and that people who work in the popularization of science are often more evangelical about the subject than are the actual practitioners.[7] Members of the so-called New Age movements are not infrequently critical of both science and the Christian faith, seeing irrevocable links between them and blaming them both for environmental crisis. This is based on the idea that science could have developed only in a society which accepted the general tenets of the Christian faith.

The mid-nineteenth-century controversy surrounding Darwin's publications has long been cited as a classic example of theological intransigence in the face of scientific developments. However, it seems that the circumstances surrounding this dispute have been misrepresented down the years and that the debate between science and theology was far from central to the discussions at the time. Despite this misunderstanding having been apparent for over fifty years, the controversy is still cited by those who seek to prolong the divide between the two disciplines or who fail to understand the issues which are involved in this debate.[8] The case of Darwin serves as an example of the mixed motives which surround the subject in general.[9]

When Darwin published his conclusions on the natural selection of species in 1859, he expected the opposition to his ideas to come from the scientists of his day rather than the leaders of the church and his expectations were realized. The strong scientific opposition to his work occurred because his conclusions damaged the vested interests of a large number of distinguished scientific figures of the time.[10] Darwin's work threatened to change the way in which people understood the world. In theological circles it was widely acknowledged that change was overdue and that the time was ripe for theological development, but no-one dared to be the first person in Britain to make such a move. The opposition which Darwin encountered from William Wilberforce, the then Bishop of Oxford, had more to do with Wilberforce's personal ambitions than with his theological objections. Wilberforce needed an easy target against which he could demonstrate his theological orthodoxy as well as raise his profile, and Darwin appeared to satisfy his need. In later years, commentators noted the opposition which was voiced by Wilberforce and rightly attacked his approach to the debate, but failed to recognize and comment on the fact that the strongest opposition was voiced by many of Darwin's fellow scientists who could not tolerate a change in the status quo. We should also note that Darwin's work was published just three months before *Essays and Reviews*, a collection of theological papers which caused the greatest theological controversy to occur in the Church of England during the nineteenth century. In the context of the generally hostile reaction to this collection, the work of Darwin inevitably became caught up in the criticism.

Since the mid-nineteenth century the debate has moved on, and more detailed discussions of the theological implications of cosmology and modern physics have become commonplace. However, all these discussions involve presuppositions of the underlying relationship which exists between science and religious belief and it is not always clear that the differences in opinions which exist between the proponents of different views are usually caused by differences in their understanding of this fundamental relationship. We shall therefore now consider the possible options which exist for this relationship and discuss the presuppositions which underlie the work in this book.

2.2 The Nature of the Relationship

From a philosophical point of view, a number of different relationships between science and religious belief are possible. These depend partly on the way in which we understand episte-mology and partly on our opinion concerning the content of religious faith and the results of scientific studies. Similar considerations dictate that there is more than one way in which this diversity of opinion can be ordered so as to form a coherent pattern. However, when discussing these relationships it is important to remember that we are drawing on the work of three different disciplines, not merely two. In addition to using the insights of science and religion we are also drawing upon the results of philosophy, and any conclusions which we produce will say something about our philosophical position as well as about our understanding of religious belief and science.

Arthur Peacocke has discussed the way in which this relationship can be considered in terms of four different dimen-sions, each of which can be further divided depending on whether the relationship is positive or negative. The first of these dimensions considers science and religion as two approaches to reality. These can either interact with each other and be mutually enriching or else they can be non-interactive and exclusive. The second dimension treats science and religion as two different language systems, each with their own rules. A third possibility is that they are generated by different attitudes which could either conflict or else be mutually compatible. Finally, there is the possibility that science and religion are each subservient to their own 'object' of study and are defined in relationship to this object.[11]

In discussing whether these relationships are positive or negative, we should note that rather than making such a sharp distinction, each dimension should be viewed on a sliding scale between these two extremes. Any given relationship would then occupy a position in a four-dimensional space defined by these four axes.

An alternative and simpler classification, which is potentially more helpful in the present study, is that given by Ian Barbour. In this classification there are four possible ways of relating science and religion which Barbour has entitled, 'independence', 'conflict', 'integration' and 'dialogue'.[12] We shall consider each of these four positions in turn, although we shall consider them in a different order to that of Barbour, and add our own observations and conclusions in each case.

Independence

Of the four positions this is possibly the easiest to understand but also the least interesting. According to this understanding, science and religion are two totally separate disciplines and they deal with totally separate items and issues. Each discipline has its own distinctive methods and uses different language systems to address its own areas of competence. Beyond those areas of competence each discipline can say nothing. There can be no conflict or dialogue between science and religion other than to discuss and decide on how to define their own mutually exclusive areas of competence.

In simple terms, the methodology of science might be thought competent to address the human exploration of the natural world, whereas that of religion is competent to deal with matters which are revealed by God. In Christian neo-orthodoxy these are what would be termed *Historie* and *Geschichte* respectively. In terms of language games, one viewpoint might be that science asks questions about natural phenomena, correlates data and makes predictions but is not competent to provide an overall worldview, a philosophy of life or an ethical standpoint. Religion, however, can provide a way of life and suggest ethical positions but is not competent to pronounce on the reasons for natural phenomena.

Although there is a degree of superficial truth in this position, in that science tends to be about the questions of 'how?' and religion the questions of 'why?', life is not compartmentalized in this simple way. The complexities of daily living are not this neat. There is also a danger in this approach, in that it incorporates a defensive attitude on the part of religion. As the sphere of influence exercised by religion under this regime is continually eroded, so it becomes an excuse to compartmentalize religion by certain scientists who wish that religion would simply go away. If this position were to be true, then although there could never be any conflict between science and religion there could also never be any constructive dialogue or mutual enrichment and insight. If this position were to be accepted, then the whole purpose of the present enquiry would be invalid and the investigation void. There would be no way forwards and no more work on the relationship between science and religion should ever be published.

Conflict

Although the position of independence is perhaps the least interesting of the relationships between science and religious belief, that of conflict is the least productive. Whilst two independent disciplines may not be able to inform each other, they are at least able to discuss their boundaries and to pursue their own business within those boundaries. However, two disciplines which are in conflict cannot even attend to their own field of study without their results being attacked from a fundamentally different standpoint based on presuppositions which are totally alien to the work in question and fail to take it seriously.

In this relationship of conflict, science and religion are understood as being fundamentally opposed to each other. This is the formal version of the popular belief that science and religion exist in a constant state of war. However, there are always two sides in a conflict and it is not unusual to find fault on both of them. In this case, the two sides of the conflict are both based on versions of fundamentalism; in the one case religious fundamentalism and in the other a scientific fundamentalism, in which science takes on the form of a quasi-religious set of beliefs.

Religious fundamentalism comes into conflict with science through its literal understanding of the Bible and its opposition to any scientific statement which contradicts or appears to cast doubt on any part of the biblical text. At its most extreme, it therefore rejects modern geology, cosmology and any form of evolution because they do not agree with the way in which it understands the accounts of the origin of the world which are provided in the opening chapters of the book of Genesis. One version of such fundamentalism has resulted in the development of so-called creation science which claims that there is scientific evidence for the biblical accounts of creation. In some ways this is a return to the position which prevailed in the early nineteenth century when geological proofs of the flood were not uncommon.[13]

Such religious fundamentalism is a threat to both scientific and religious freedom. It denies the ability of science to investigate the natural world and it also dictates that religious belief should follow a particular rigid pattern. Indeed, through its rejection of the results of scientific investigations, it can attempt to impose its beliefs on people against their will. Such a totalitarian approach is actually an enemy of true religion because those who live outside the religious community can come to believe that this is the only way in which religion operates and therefore reject religion entirely or treat it as a subject of ridicule. Such reactions are not uncommon in Western society at the present time.

Religious fundamentalism is also an enemy of religion when it circumscribes those within the religious community and either makes them afraid to question its claims for fear of being excluded or else closes their minds to the ability of God to act in a new way. It becomes the result of the decision of a self-selected group of people that they and they alone are correct. Although a full discussion is beyond the scope of the present work, it should be noted that even in the infamous case of Galileo and his condemnation by the church, the issues were not those of a conflict between science and religion, but far more complex in nature.[14]

However, fundamentalism is not confined to religion. Scientific materialism makes assertions for science which are similar to those which religious fundamentalism makes about its particular set of beliefs. In this case we can find the belief that scientific methodology (as defined by the fundamentalists) is the only reliable path to knowledge of any kind and that matter is the fundamental reality of the universe. As with religious fundamentalism, there are various levels of sophistication within this approach. In its crudest forms, its adherents seem to be unaware that the universe does not obey the rules of classical physics and that it is not possible to prove the existence of the physical world independent of the observer. More sophisticated proponents of scientific fundamentalism are well aware of the methods and results of modern science but choose to use them in such a way as to actively discredit religious belief.

If this position of conflict is taken to be correct then once again there is little hope for the present study as the two disciplines will not be able to listen to each other and consider any similarities in their position. This book is written from the perspective that conflict between science and religion is unnecessary and that its presence both does a disservice to and belittles the work of both disciplines. It occurs when the proponents of either science or a particular faith fail to attempt to understand the views and understandings of the other. This also means that both scientific and religious fundamentalism should be rejected. As we shall see in section 2.3, there are a number of distinct similarities in the methods of science and religion. This in itself lends weight to the argument that it is unnecessary for them to find themselves in conflict.

Integration

On first consideration, this could be thought of as potentially the most productive of the four possible relationships discussed by Barbour. It denies any separation between science and religion and understands them as two different aspects of the same enterprise. As such, its understanding of epistemology is very different from the position of independence and its conclusions are totally rejected by those who hold a fundamentalist position. Indeed, a fundamentalist would feel betrayed by such an approach – a Christian fundamentalist would probably deny that anyone taking such a position could possibly be a Christian.

According to Ian Barbour there are several distinct versions of integration.[15] He firstly identifies natural theology, in which God is inferred from design and through human reason rather than through His own self-revelation. The appearance of the universe itself proves God. Secondly, Barbour identifies a theology of nature in which the results of scientific investigation lead to a reformulation of Christian doctrine so that the two are compatible. Such a reformulation is based on considerations of how God acts in the world, which is believed to be through law and chance. Finally, Barbour suggests that it might be possible to develop a systematic synthesis or all-encompassing theory which can deal with everything, including the religious aspects of life. An example of such a theory would be process theology in which all things are thought to be related and in which any change has the effect of changing all things. Both a theology of nature and process theology are compatible with various forms of panentheism in which the universe is seen as being a part (but not the whole) of God – literally, the universe is within God.[16]

If our considerations of the Second Law of Thermodynamics and Original Sin lead to the conclusion that there are parallels between these two subjects, then this could be taken as evidence to support the suggestion that integration is a valid proposal. If God does indeed lie behind everything in the universe, then integration would presumably be the correct way in which to understand the relationship. However, it seems at present that neither our scientific methods nor our religious beliefs are amenable to such a combination. Barbour has presented objections to each of the three positions suggested above, including the observation that the route to integration via natural theology leads to deism – the belief that there is a God – and not to the personal God of Love who is worshipped in the Christian faith, and whom we describe as Trinity.

Russell Stannard has noted that despite the similarities which do exist between scientific and theological methods, there are also a number of ways in which the two enterprises are quite distinct.[17] Not least of these is that science deals largely with what is impersonal whilst Christianity is inherently personal in its nature. Perhaps the truth is that both science and religious beliefs are part of a larger whole and whilst in this sense they can be integrated, this is not an integration which can be understood at the present time. This is certainly consistent with the religious assertion of the *via negativa* which claims that we cannot say anything about God which we know to be absolutely true, as well as the *via positiva* which claims that it is better to say something which we know to be partial than to say nothing at all. If both science and religion are (separate) parts of a greater whole then it is likely that the most productive and fruitful way to examine their relationship is through the consideration of the dialogue which would then exist between them.

Dialogue

The premise that the relationship between science and religion is one of dialogue implies that the two disciplines overlap with each other and have parallels. They have an interacting approach to reality which implies that they can inform each other through their complementary considerations of related issues. The origins of this dialogue perhaps lie in the origins and development of science itself, although this should not be considered as a proof but rather regarded as supporting the working hypothesis.

It is generally agreed that the development of science required the belief or assumption that the universe is both ordered and contingent.[18] Such a belief need not have been stated explicitly but was implicit in the development of the scientific enterprise. The universe needed to be ordered so that general theories could be produced which would work in all situations at all times. The universe also needed to be contingent so that these general theories could be deduced only by investigation rather than from first principles by processes of logic and philosophy – the universe did not have to be the way it is.

The ancient Greeks presupposed that the universe was ordered and consistent, but also presupposed that there was a necessity about this order so that information could all be deduced through mental processes. In contrast, the pre-Hellenic Jewish culture believed in contingency, but had no concept of continuous operation of natural laws within the world.[19] The argument can then be advanced that it was only in the Judeo-Christian world (which had of course been influenced by Greek culture) that acceptance of both order and contingency made scientific development possible.[20] Natural science can be seen as the child of the order which is present in the philosophy of Greek culture and the contingency which is present in Jewish religious beliefs. These conditions were met in the Christian faith.

This does not mean that religious belief is necessary for someone to be a successful scientist any more than they need to be an expert in Greek philosophy. However, if this account of scientific origins is true, even if only in part, then it throws further doubt on arguments that religion and science should be in conflict or that they are wholly separate enterprises. It is more likely that they are related and have the ability to communicate with each other if only each of them would be prepared to listen to what the other is saying. Indeed, of the four options, it is dialogue which allows traditional religious doctrines to function in the physical world as described by science. Integration would require that both science and religion need to change (which might be the case). However, conflict requires that either the results of scientific enquiry or those of religion must be denied, and independence allows religious thought no contact with the scientific view of the world.

We should also note Polkinghorne's observation that dialogue comes in a wide spectrum of opinions and that he therefore subdivides it into four distinct theological positions which he terms 'deistic', 'theistic', 'revisionary' and 'developmental'.[21] In the deistic approach, dialogue is limited and God is understood as some form of cosmic intelligence unattached to any particular world faith, as exemplified by the work of Paul Davies.[22] The theistic approach moves on to include worship and practice within a particular religious tradition but without taking on board the full range of doctrine. Polkinghorne sees Ian Barbour as a leading proponent of this position. The revisionary approach, as demonstrated by Arthur Peacocke, seeks to revise the content of a particular faith system in the light of scientific teaching. The developmental approach, into which Polkinghorne places himself, pictures the interaction between science and theology as a continuously unfolding exploration. However, as Polkinghorne puts it, 'Religious beliefs describe reality and have a givenness in their core doctrine which is not open to revision.'[23]

Polkinghorne notes that science has a cumulative attainment, whereas theology – like many other human disciplines – does not. Different theologians write and think at different times in history but that does not make the thinking or the writing of those who have come more recently any more advanced than that of those who worked hundreds of years ago. It is worth noting that the present author places himself firmly within this developmental approach and that it therefore underlies the present study.

It will be clear from this discussion that the position of dialogue is the current favorite, at least for the present author. However, whilst dialogue is probably the most generally helpful and constructive of Barbour's four stances, we should be beware of making it the exclusive position. We can quite easily conceive of a spectrum of stances which covers the ground of all four, as well as the ground in between. Moreover, to state that 'this is the relationship' is to take an essentialist standpoint and to miss the fact that all four have been adopted at various times and in various circumstances and that more than one may play an important role in the relationship.[24] Whatever our approach, we must also be aware of the problems created by the use of a methodology which involves a 'God of the gaps' – the use of God to explain those areas of knowledge which have not yet yielded to human research. In the past this approach was often used in a rather crude manner and ran the repeated and oft-demonstrated risk that the latest advance in scientific knowledge could annul theological claims. Today, although this approach is still used in a crude form by religious fundamentalists, it is also used unwittingly in more sophisticated arguments where its presence may not be immediately apparent to the author concerned. There is always the risk that we use God to fill gaps in our knowledge and understanding, with the result that as such knowledge and understanding increase, so God's realm grows smaller. However, any God worthy of our worship is the God of all and not merely of the gaps. He is to be found through all things and is to be experienced in the everyday objects which we use and in the people whom we meet as we go about our daily lives. Charles Coulson was quite clear that God is not a God of the gaps and that God should not be used in this way.[25]

We shall proceed on the assumption that scientific enquiry and religious belief exist in dialogue, although we must also be open to the possibility that another option is possible, especially that the two disciplines might be closer than we at first imagined. With this assumption in mind we shall now examine the relationship which exists between the methodologies of science and theology.

2.3 Similarities in Methodology

At first sight it might be supposed that scientific research and theological endeavor make use of very different methods. Whenever I try to explain that the methods which I use in theology are very similar to those which I formerly used in science, the usual reaction is one of incredulity. The problem is that there appears to be a widespread misunderstanding about the way in which modern science goes about its business. Indeed, it could be argued that there is almost a complete ignorance about scientific method, and it is certainly this misunderstanding which leads to the commonly held but erroneous belief that 'science disproves religion'.[26] In general terms this misunderstanding makes four assumptions, each of which is largely correct for the objects which we encounter in everyday life but which break down when we look at small-scale objects in detail.

The first of these assumptions is that the theories which we construct in science correspond exactly to material objects in the real world. The second is that things have an existence which is independent of our presence, and the third that these things existed prior to our thinking about them. Finally, there is the assumption that we can describe material objects exactly as they are. This overall misunderstanding is a form of realism or positivism and corresponds approximately to the scientific understanding of the universe which existed prior to the twentieth century, although even then there were a number of other philosophical positions concerning our acquisition of knowledge. The misunderstanding has been summarized in terms of classical physics by Russell Stannard.[27]

When these tenets of what is now termed 'classical realism' are applied to the world, then they produce what could be termed the 'supposedly classical' scientific method. In this method, any observations which are made by an observer yield information about the world which enable the observer to construct hypotheses about that world. If these hypotheses can then be verified through further experimentation, they become theories which are thought to describe the world as it actually is. Despite the fact that this is not how most practicing scientists seem to work or believe that they work, it is a view which is widely propounded, especially by popularizers of science. It also appears to be an underlying assumption of the way in which science is often taught in schools.

Crucial to this classical method is the principal of verification, which states that we must obtain positive proof that an hypothesis is correct if it is to be accepted as a scientific fact. However, it is now widely accepted that this is not how the scientific method works at all. Karl Popper argued that rather than verification being the key point, hypotheses should be considered in terms of the principal of falsification. A valid hypothesis or theory must be open to the possibility of being shown to be false, but it is generally held to be a valid description of reality until the time when such falsification occurs. This often happens through the inability of the hypothesis to explain new or additional data. Even if the results of experimentation continually agree with the hypothesis over a long period of time, this cannot constitute a valid proof of the hypothesis, as an alternative hypothesis could still provide equally good agreement and further results could still result in its falsification. Indeed, according to this principle, any valid hypothesis must be constructed in such a way that it could be falsified. Such an approach is incompatible with any form of fundamentalism, which is by its very nature not open to dialogue or to being disproved.

It is unfortunate that this point is not more widely appreciated. In his otherwise excellent discussion of the subject, Tom Wright misses out on this point. When he examines the methodology used by historians, he notes that the 'historical method is just like all other methods of enquiry. It proceeds by means of "hypotheses" which stand in need of "verification"'.[28] It appears that in this discussion Wright has missed the point about falsification.

The idea that nothing can be regarded as being true until it has been verified is a basic tenet of logical positivism. However, logical positivism is now generally discredited, not least because it cannot satisfy its own basic tenet that all hypotheses must be verified if they are to be accepted as fact. It is itself a hypothesis which cannot be verified. According to logical positivism, God cannot exist because He cannot be verified. However, as logical positivism itself cannot be verified this argument is hardly conclusive. Moreover, as the methods of classical realism are incapable of describing the physical world, it is hardly surprising that they are unable to verify the existence of God. Classical realism and logical positivism do not generally describe the way in which we live. As John Polkinghorne observes, most people tend to live their lives trusting in their experience until it is found to mislead them, rather than going around asking for proof of everything which they encounter.[29] There are few people around who understand much of the detail as to how personal computers, radios and televisions work, with the result that most of us simply take the results on trust and simply get on with the business of using them.

If the above picture painted by realism occupies one end of the epistemological spectrum, then the opposite end is occupied by the ideas of instrumentalism. In instrumentalism all theories are taken to be wholly human constructs. It is claimed that although these theories may well be of utility, in that they can be used to rationalize data, they are actually a total fiction which bears no necessary correspondence to reality. This is an extreme application of the fact that we cannot describe anything exactly as it is. Whenever we observe an object, then the observations which we chose to make are determined by our presuppositions about the object under consideration, and these presuppositions also color the content of what we observe. Our very act of observation itself alters that which we are observing. As such, it is possible to meet philosophers and physicists who do not believe that the physical world exists.[30]

Most scientists actually carry out their work without bothering to worry about the philosophical description of what it is that they are doing; like travelers on a road, they are unworried by philosophers who debate whether or not the road exists or whether it should lead in a different direction. Nevertheless, the most commonly accepted view of their methodology is now taken to be that described by critical realism. Critical realism accepts that although theories cannot be deduced objectively from data, because there are always presuppositions involved in collecting and interpreting the data, the theories which are produced do nevertheless point to a reality which existed prior to the theory and beyond the observer. All data and observations involve the observer's presuppositions, and the theories which result from reflection on the data are therefore partial representations of a greater reality. These theories should be used as aids to understanding, rather than portrayed as the absolute truth, albeit that they do contain an interpretation of that truth. This method is described as 'realism' because it maintains that there is a reality 'out there' which is open to our investigation and which we can describe, albeit with some degree of imperfection, but it is also 'critical' because it acknowledges that the results of our investigations are always provisional and subject to revision.

It is worth noting that Alister McGrath has constructed what he describes as a 'critically real theology' based upon scientific methodology. This is a valid approach since theology has long borrowed the methodologies of other academic or philosophical disciplines, notably those of Plato and Aristotle, and by adopting this approach McGrath has produced work of major significance. However, it is not surprising that this is the case because both science and theology should both describe the actual world.

These three positions of realism, instrumentalism and critical realism also apply to theology and religious belief. The strict realist is akin to the fundamentalist who believes that it is possible to obtain absolute and unalterable knowledge about God. Indeed, this is the realist view of God – a God who exists beyond doubt and about whom we can have absolute knowledge – although the sources of knowledge involved here are very different to those of a scientific realist. In religious terms, the instrumentalist is a non-realist who believes in a non-real God who is solely the product of his own mind. The critical realist is like the person who, to paraphrase the words of St Paul, 'looks through a glass darkly' with the hope and expectation that one day they will see face to face.[31] Writers who promote the understanding that science and religion should exist in dialogue also tend to promote the understanding that both religion and science approach the world via critical realism. Arthur Peacocke maintains that the outcome of such critical realism is the hypothesis that science and religion are interacting approaches to reality.[32] Both science and theology engage with realities which may be referred to, but which are beyond a totally literal description. If we adapt a critically real approach to both science and theology then it is wholly appropriate to ask how the contents of these two respective fields of study might be related to each other.

One possibility is that if the above claims about critical realism are true then the beliefs of a religious system correspond to the hypotheses and theories of a scientific system. As such, both religious beliefs and scientific hypotheses need to follow similar rules or to satisfy comparable criteria if they are to be taken seriously. Different authors formulate such rules or criteria in different ways. The four criteria given below are taken from the account given by Barbour who usefully compares their application in both science and religion.[33]

Firstly, any theory or belief must take account of all the available and relevant data which is generally accepted as being reliable by the practitioners in the field concerned. We cannot pick and choose our data at will, but have to include all the available data which is relevant. If the belief or theory does not satisfy this criterion and fails to agree with all the data then it is likely to be flawed. A relevant example of a good theory would be the way in which the Second Law of Thermodynamics appears to apply to all chemical systems under the conditions which are encountered in a chemistry laboratory. Within Christian theology, we could make the claim that the universal failure of human beings to live perfect lives is consistent with a belief in Original Sin.

Secondly, the hypothesis or belief must paint a coherent picture which makes sense of the data and is consistent with other theories which impinge on the subject under consideration. For example, the Second Law of Thermodynamics not only makes sense of the energy changes which occur during chemical processes, but in combination with other theories enables us to make predictions which were beyond its original scope. An example of such a prediction would be the voltage produced by an electrochemical cell. In the Christian faith the doctrine of Original Sin is consistent with both the doctrine of the atonement (what Jesus achieved through His crucifixion – see Chapter 4) and the doctrine of the incarnation (God appearing in human form).

Thirdly, a good theory will offer a wide scope or perspective and may draw together areas of study which were previously believed to be separate. Historically, the Second Law of Thermodynamics explained why many chemical reactions are irreversible as well as why certain chemical processes can occur even though they need to absorb heat from their surroundings in order to happen. Either alone or in combination with other theories, the Second Law of Thermodynamics lies behind a wide range of apparently diverse areas of chemistry. In theological terms, the doctrine of Original Sin can play its part in holding together a range of different areas of thought which could otherwise be interpreted as having little relationship with each other. This is particularly the case when considering ethical issues and human nature, and the way in which they can be related to our understanding of God. A further theological example is the way in which the doctrine of the Trinity itself is increasingly being seen as vital in providing links between different areas of doctrine.[34]

Fourthly, the theory or belief must be fruitful in that it can help us to understand new data as this becomes available and can also help us to select those subjects which are worthy of future study. In a religious context, a belief might be judged on the basis of its ability to change a person's character or lifestyle. The Second Law of Thermodynamics has proved itself in understanding the complexities of systems which display local order, such as liquid crystals. In the case of the doctrine of Original Sin, the present study may serve to demonstrate the way in which ideas can sometimes prove fruitful in unexpected ways. This fourth stage also includes the important possibility that an established hypothesis could be found wanting because of the emergence of new data which it cannot explain. This is the principle of falsification which we have already examined above. However, it is necessary to proceed with caution when considering such falsification for, as Polkinghorne notes, all 'high-level' theories encounter a certain amount of opposition.[35] The real test is whether this opposition constitutes a serious challenge to the theory in question or whether it merely results in minor modifications. Of course, over the years, such modifications can build up to the point where the theory is no longer tenable; see section 2.4 below.

The principle of falsification which is implicit in much scientific research shows the error of searching for positive proof in any religious quest. Provided that our beliefs satisfy the four criteria discussed above, then they are valid until such time as they are shown to be false. Judging by the profusion of books produced by theologians during the second half of the twentieth century there is no problem with Christian beliefs being unfruitful. The only problem with this could be that Christian beliefs might be open to falsification only through an experience which occurs beyond the death of the individual. This is especially true if we accept Polkinghorne's observation that 'high-level' theories always encounter opposition, a fact to which the Christian faith bears witness.

However, the similarity in the approach of the two disciplines extends beyond this four-part methodology. There is also what we might term a much 'softer' point of comparison which only emerges as researchers discuss the way in which they feel about their work. By its very nature, Christian theology is influenced to a certain extent by considerations of aesthetics and the elegance of its arguments and discussions. It has often been argued that such considerations are absent from science[36] but this is not the case. I know from personal experience of the delight to be derived from the elegance of an experiment or theoretical expression and the way in which what later came to be seen as the right result often contained a certain beauty or symmetry.

Bishop David Walker has recounted to me how his research into pure mathematics needed to have aesthetic qualities in order to be acceptable to his supervisors. Both science and theological discourse are also influenced by economics and politics and, as we shall see in Chapter 6, the sociological and psychological similarities between the two fields are closer than we might at first think.

The present contention is therefore that both science and religion are directed towards the search for understanding and truth. They are both concerned with discovering and describing the nature of reality. However, in this search it is important that they both recognize that they have their limitations. The theories and beliefs which they produce do actually refer to something but they can never be the whole story. All data are influenced by theories or presuppositions (they are said to be 'theory-laden'), even if these only amount to the decision to collect or examine certain types of data as opposed to others. There is a circularity in the search for knowledge which cannot be avoided.[37] Given these parallels, it is pertinent to ask how science and religion both contribute to describing the same world.

2.4 Describing One World

It sometimes seems that both scientific and Christian fundamentalists seek to exploit any perceptible difference between Christianity and science as a means of attacking what they appear to understand as a discipline which stands in opposition to their own. Meanwhile, scientists who are Christians carry on with their work as scientists, and Christians who live in a world of scientific products carry on with their lives and use the outcomes of scientific endeavor as if the possibility of a conflict had never occurred to them.

The present contention is that the behavior of such fundamentalists is disturbing, not least because it is based on a profound misunderstanding, deliberate or otherwise, as to the nature of both science and religious belief. Such behavior needs to be opposed by those who hold a more conciliatory position, not least because the public perspective can sometimes be that such conflict is the only option available. Indeed, there is a definite strangeness about the stance taken by a religious fundamentalist who nevertheless regularly uses and relies upon the products of those sciences which have only been made possible by a rejection of a part of the worldview to which he subscribes. More subtly, there is also a certain irony in a scientific fundamentalist rejecting the Christian faith out of hand when it may well be true that it was the rise of Christianity, with its combination of Jewish and Greek ideas giving the picture of an ordered but contingent universe, which allowed the development of modern science in the first place.

The behavior both of scientists who are active members of the Christian church and of Christians who make use of science in their daily lives, is only acceptable provided that they are aware of what they are doing. Their lifestyle is making the statement that both science and religious belief have a part to play in daily life. It is very worrying if a stance in which the two fields are mentally compartmentalized and kept separate is adopted as a defense against a possible erosion of faith, and profoundly sad if this defense has been adopted because of pressure from those who hold fundamentalist positions. It is also vitally important that there are people who do pay attention to the similarities between the two fields. Those people who seek to drive a wedge between science and Christianity must not be allowed to have matters all their own way, and the voice of those who work happily within both disciplines needs to be heard a great deal more than it is at present, particularly in the public forum. In this context, however, it is important to address the question as to whether scientific and religious worldviews are reconcilable or whether there is an irreconcilable difference between them.

In section 1.3 we examined one possible version of the

Christian worldview. In philosophical terms, such a worldview could be said to constitute a paradigm, that is, a self-consistent set of presuppositions which define our all-embracing understanding of everything around us. A paradigm defines the questions which can be asked and determines the sort of answers which can be received. As an example, the idea that the universe is orderly and contingent could be considered to be the basic scientific paradigm. As we noted in section 2.2, science makes the assumption that the universe is orderly, with the same physical laws applying at all times and in all places. If physical laws operate differently at different times or places then the scientific paradigm fails and scientific methodology is no longer possible. Because each paradigm is self-consistent it is possible for different paradigms to come into conflict with each other. Because of this internal self-consistency, such conflicts cannot be resolved from within the given paradigms and by definition there is no higher authority which lies beyond and which is shared by the different paradigms. An example of such a conflict would be that which can occur between scientific and religious fundamentalism. It is important to remember that in the present work we are using the word 'paradigm' in an all-embracing sense as it is a term which has become devalued and misunderstood through its use to describe any package of ideas which are often of limited scope.[38]

A paradigm is closely related to what Imre Lakatos has called a 'research programme'.[39] This is again a self-consistent set of ideas, as discussed above, but now a distinction is drawn between what is regarded as the core set of ideas, which are not open to negotiation or change, and the auxiliary ideas within which modification is possible without any alteration to the core ideas. Such a description ties in well with the falsification principle which was discussed in section 2.3 above, because the falsification of auxiliary ideas need not destroy the main hypothesis and it may be possible to produce new auxiliary ideas which allow the retention of core material or which may actually strengthen its position. This approach provides a more satisfactory account of both scientific and religious enquiry than the simple falsification of a paradigm which we have examined above. A good example of this principle is the way in which Newtonian mechanics could not explain the motion of the planet Uranus. Rather than abandon Newtonian mechanics, a new auxiliary hypothesis was added, proposing the existence of a further planet. In due course Neptune was detected, and Newtonian mechanics survived.

However, the cost in auxiliary ideas can sometimes become too great and the core program then has to be abandoned. A further step in the use of Newtonian mechanics to explain the solar system concerned unexplained discrepancies in the motion of the planet Mercury. This time, the auxiliary hypothesis of an additional unobserved planet proved less satisfactory and the situation was not resolved until the core program of Newtonian mechanics was replaced by Einstein's theories of relativity.

The historical development of physical chemistry and thermodynamics is full of further examples in which the initial formulae used to explain physical and chemical properties were later found to be inaccurate and were therefore modified by the addition of auxiliary equations. Later still, it was sometimes the case that the whole formula was abandoned and replaced by a totally new expression. A good example of such a change concerns the equation of state for a gas; the equation which describes the mutual relationship between its pressure, volume and temperature.[40]

This idea of such research programs can apply to both science and to religious belief. In religious terms such a paradigm or research program may be the whole of a religion, such as Christianity or Hinduism. Alternatively, it might be considered that within the Christian faith evangelical fundamentalism and radical non-realism have so little in common that they therefore constitute separate paradigms. Such an illustration raises the question as to what would be considered to be the core ideas in Christianity if it is indeed to be regarded as a research program in the way defined by Lakatos.

If science and religion do exist in dialogue with each other, then it should be clear from the above discussion that there must be a certain amount of common ground to their research programs as well as no necessary conflict between their core ideas. If the Christian worldview proposed by Wright and summarized in section 1.3 is taken as a valid statement of Christian belief, then the parallels in language between Sin and the Second Law of Thermodynamics could be vital in supporting the hypothesis that there is no necessary conflict between this worldview and that of mainstream science. If we look closely and thoughtfully at their relationship, we may well find that science and Christianity are closer than most people care to believe.

It is important to understand that this is not an attempt to prove that there is no conflict or that the two worldviews are essentially the same as each other. It is rather a demonstration that neither view can necessarily falsify the other and that both of these worldviews, or paradigms, can continue to exist in dialogue. They both explain the data and there is no necessary conflict. Such a dialogue is not about apologetics, either of science to Christianity or Christianity to science, but about a mutual exploration of each discipline by the other. Just as in a good marriage neither partner is dominant or exploitative, so it should be in this relationship. Verification is not possible in either area of study, and our interest should lie in enrichment and understanding, for that is what dialogue should be about.

An example of the way in which uncertainties and apologetics can be misused in this debate concerns the subject of reductionism. Scientists are divided as to whether or not the properties of complex systems can always be predicted from the properties of their components, provided that we have access to sufficient information about the system concerned and a powerful enough computer to carry out the necessary calculations. If, in principle, such calculations are possible, then this is termed 'reductionism'. In simple terms it would involve the belief that the properties of quarks could be used to predict the properties of subatomic particles which could in turn be used to predict the properties of atoms. From here, the properties of all molecules could be calculated and these could be used to make predictions about living cells which would themselves relate to the properties of living organisms, and so on. In essence, this is to claim that the whole of biology can be predicted from chemistry and physics and that all chemistry can be predicted from nuclear physics.

Such reductionism can move on from being a natural and understandable scientific methodology into a genuine philosophical belief that this process is ultimately possible. Indeed, for scientists such as Richard Dawkins, reductionism becomes an anti-religious crusade with the presupposition that there is no meaning or purpose to the universe and that only science can produce a proper explanation of anything.[41]

Arthur Peacocke, John Polkinghorne and Ian Barbour all believe that the predictions ultimately claimed for reductionism are not possible.[42] Polkinghorne notes that molecular biologists such as Francis Crick are more prone to such claims than are physicists who, after eighteenth-century moves in this direction, have become more cautious. This greater reluctance to accept reductionism on the part of physicists is all the more telling because they work with lower-level systems than do biologists. It is not an uncommon stance to suppose that complex systems exhibit genuine novelty and that the behavior of their parts is not simply the sum or a predictable combination of their isolated behaviors. There is something extra which is present in a living cell and which cannot be predicted from the properties of the molecules alone, and the same appears to apply to arrays of crystals such as superconductors. Such unpredictable properties are sometimes described as 'holistic' features and the universe is said to demonstrate 'level autonomy' in which each level of complexity has its own separateness.

Unfortunately, discussions on reductionism can involve ulterior motives. It is not unusual for level autonomy to be used as a proof for God in an argument which is akin to that of the 'God of the gaps', an argument in which God is used to account for gaps in human knowledge and understanding. For example, John Polkinghorne has produced a sophisticated argument in favor of God which is based upon the supply of information.[43] Although this argument is clearly not intended to be a version of the 'God of the gaps' argument in any naive sense, it has been criticized on the grounds that it effectively constitutes such an approach. It is also possible to find arguments in favor of reductionism which appear to be motivated by a desire to banish all thoughts of God from the discussion. This occurs not only in the arguments of authors such as Richard Dawkins, which are at least explicit, but also in contexts where a writer in a scientific journal attacks a scientifically anti-reductionist stance purely on anti-religious grounds.[44] There is a need for honesty in accepting the motivation which may lie behind our arguments as well as care in the way in which these arguments are presented.

The core issue which lies behind this discussion is that of indeterminacy and whether we can attain to total knowledge. At present there are clearly gaps in what it is possible for us to know, and we need to examine the cause of these gaps. Such indeterminacy could be due to one of three factors. Firstly, it could be caused by temporary human ignorance, so that when we devise new scientific theories or develop more sophisticated scientific instruments or computers the indeterminacy will disappear. Secondly, it could be due to inherent experimental or conceptual limitations. The information is present but there is no way in which it can be extracted from the system. Thirdly, it is possible that there is an inherent indeterminacy in the nature of the universe.

These three possibilities can be correlated to our understanding of epistemology. The first corresponds to classical realism since it embodies the claim that ultimately it is possible to know everything. The second corresponds to instrumentalism as it carries the promise that we cannot know the nature of reality. The third fits with critical realism, because although we can obtain information about the object of our studies, such information will always be only part of the story because the whole story is never present, no matter however hard we look.[45]

The present contention follows Barbour in commending the path of critical realism and maintains that the whole story is never present. A dialogue between different paradigms is likely to include more of the material than is ever possible within a single paradigm but it will still not be the complete story. This is completely consistent with Polkinghorne's adoption of a developmental model within the dialogue, through which new possibilities continually unfold. For the scientist, this is a part of the continual unfolding of our understanding of the universe. In terms of Christian spirituality, both the *via positiva* and the *via negativa* have their roles to play, and a theologian might say that this is consistent with the God who makes all things new. Ultimately, both science and theology should oppose the claims of those who claim to know the whole of the story, whatever their perspective or presuppositions, as well as the views of those who claim that the story cannot exist in the first place. Scientists and theologians should both insist on the difficult but essential quest to search for the truth and recognize that, although their searches are not identical, they do have similarities and there can be value and a great deal to be learned in talking to the travelers whom they meet on the way.

Sin and the Second Law

Death is a natural and unavoidable aspect of the world in which we live. If we examine the life of an individual plant or animal in any detail, then it becomes quite apparent that there is an ageing process at work and that this ageing will eventually result in the death of the individual concerned. The time scale of this process varies from species to species. It may be a few days in the case of some insects or hundreds of years in the case of certain species of tree, but natural death as the result of ageing is always the final result. Premature death, whether from disease, accident or natural disaster, simply ends a particular life more rapidly than otherwise would have been the case. This premature death may be tragic, but in terms of our present arguments it has the same cause and the same end result as death from old age or from other natural causes. If we set aside the deliberate action of another individual or group of individuals, then death is always the result of the unremitting increase in disorder which is a part of the universe in which we live; an increase which has been labeled the Second Law of Thermodynamics.

Throughout human history the various religions have attempted to explain human mortality, and Christianity is no different. The Christian view has traditionally been that, in theological terms, the world is fallen and the death of a human being results from the presence of Sin within the world.[1] St Paul, writing to the Christian community in Rome, extended this causality to the whole creation when he noted that 'the creation itself will be set free from its bondage to decay ...'[2] Paul clearly made a connection between Sin and the mortality which affects the whole of life on earth, rather than seeing Sin simply as a human condition. If we follow the lead of Pauline theology then we die either because of Sin itself and its concomitant mortality or as a result of the sins of other people. Even so, the present claim would be that the Christian church has far too often focused its attention on a discussion about Sin, sins and our salvation from such sins, rather than on addressing the subjects of death and resurrection and the way in which we are saved from the consequences of death. As a result, the church has paid too little attention to this wider perspective. As we have seen already, James Barr believes that the creation narrative of Adam and Eve has been misread and the focus needs to shift more towards the issue of mortality. When Jesus wept following the death of His friend Lazarus, His concern was clearly with the loss of a human being rather than his moral failings.

In Chapter 1 we noted the apparent similarity between the increasing disorder of the universe as described by the Second Law of Thermodynamics and the presence of both moral and physical evil within the universe. The propensity for the human species to perform actions which fall into the category of moral evil has often been called 'Original Sin' although we have argued that the term 'Sin' itself could also be used to describe physical evil. It is now time to return to this similarity and to examine it in more detail. Is the similarity merely a coincidence, or is there an underlying truth which gives rise to both of these descriptions of the world? In order to pursue these investigations we must first pay closer attention to the Second Law of Thermodynamics and to its consequences.

3.1 The Second Law in More Detail

The Second Law of Thermodynamics describes commonplace events which happen around about us all the time. Although relatively few people might be able to describe this law in any detail, it is something which is an intuitive part of the experience of most human beings. Children learn its effects at an early age even if they are unaware that these effects have all been summarized into a general scientific statement. They learn that hot and cold water mix to form warm water, but that warm water does not spontaneously divide itself up to produce hot and cold water. They learn that ornaments break when they are dropped onto a hard surface but that the reverse, unfortunately, does not happen – the ornament will not reform from its broken pieces and then replace itself onto the shelf from which it came. They learn that raw food can be cooked and thereby change in its appearance, taste and texture but that cooked food cannot be returned to its raw state or ingredients.

These are all examples of the general rule that any spontaneous event, such as sugar dissolving in hot tea, is accompanied by an increase in disorder or entropy. In the case of an event which is not spontaneous, then the event in question must be driven along by an input of energy. If this input of energy causes a decrease in the disorder of the system where the event occurs (in other words, it becomes more ordered), then this decrease will be more than balanced by an increase in the disorder at the source of the energy. This net increase will, in turn, become an overall increase in the disorder of the universe. Turning a pile of building materials into a well-constructed and ordered house requires a great deal of physical labor which, in turn, heats up the surroundings and causes a greater amount of disorder which is distributed widely elsewhere. This principle of increasing disorder also lies behind the examples which we examined in Chapter 1, namely the burning of a log, the acceleration of a car, and a book falling from a shelf. In each case there is an increase in the total disorder of the universe. This disorder, as measured on a molecular level in which we consider the behavior of individual molecules, is what we term 'entropy'.

In the introduction to his book *The Second Law*, Henry Bent, one-time associate professor of chemistry at the University of Minnesota, describes why ice will melt at high temperatures but not at low temperatures.[3] He notes that when ice melts in warm water, the water is cooled down and its entropy, or disorder, is thereby decreased because the water molecules now move around less rapidly. However, this decrease in the disorder of the existing water is more than compensated for by the increase in disorder which occurs as the fixed water molecules from the ice are freed by the melting, so that they can then move randomly throughout the liquid water. Ice itself does not melt at low temperatures for a similar reason. Although the increase in entropy from the melting of the ice would still be present and have a similar effect to that which occurred above, the surroundings still have to supply the necessary heat, and the lower temperature means that the associated decrease in the entropy of the surroundings is now much greater. This therefore outweighs the increase which comes from the melting of the ice. The net result is that rather than cold ice melting, it is instead the case that the cold water will freeze.

When water freezes and forms ice, the water molecules themselves become more ordered and so their disorder or entropy decreases. However, the surroundings become more disordered because they are heated up by the energy released by the water as it freezes. The lower the temperature, the greater is the entropy change produced by a given amount of heat.[4] If we cool water down, there is therefore a point at which the decrease in the entropy of the water should it freeze is exactly balanced by the increase in entropy of the surroundings. The temperature at which this occurs is the melting point of ice (the freezing point of water) which occurs at zero Celsius or 273.16 degrees on the Kelvin scale. Once we reduce the temperature further, the entropy released by the heating of the surroundings outweighs the reduction in entropy in the water and it therefore turns to ice. As an aside, we should note that at zero degrees on the Kelvin scale (absolute zero or -273.16 Celsius) any substance is perfectly ordered and has a zero entropy, a statement known as the Third

Law of Thermodynamics.

In order to explore what lies behind the Second Law in more detail, it is helpful to turn to an alternative definition which we noted in Chapter 1. There we noted: *Spontaneous changes are those which, if carried out under the proper conditions, can be made to do work. If carried out reversibly they yield a maximum amount of work. In natural processes the maximum work is never obtained.* In other words, when something happens naturally, we can harness the changes which occur and extract usable energy from them. When we burn coal, the heat of combustion can be used to warm a room or to boil water and generate steam which can then be used to generate electricity. When water falls downhill the energy associated with its motion (kinetic energy) can again be used to generate electricity. Applied in the right way, electricity itself carries out many spontaneous changes such as producing light from a light bulb or driving an electric motor.

However, in each of these examples, if we measure the amount of useful energy obtained from the system, then we discover that it never adds up to the amount which went in. For example, a coal-fired power station only converts some 35 percent of the energy available from burning coal in a furnace into the electricity which the station generates for the consumer. Since energy is always conserved, a statement known as the First Law of Thermodynamics, then it is clear that around two-thirds of the available energy has been lost somewhere. This unusable or lost energy can be shown to be equal to the heat losses of the system (i.e. the warmth which escapes to the surroundings) plus the increase in entropy multiplied by the temperature at which it occurred. In practice, unless the heat losses can be recovered in some way, then as the lost energy gradually becomes distributed throughout the surroundings so this loss also eventually becomes an increase in the entropy of the universe.[5]

From the above discussion, it might be noticed that the entropy of a given system increases as that system tends to become more uniform. Ice or water by themselves (the choice depends on the temperature) have a higher entropy than a mixture of ice and water together at the same temperature and in practice either the water freezes or the ice melts. In the same way, the slightly warmer surroundings of a power station have a higher entropy than did the coal prior to its being burnt in the furnaces. These observations form a basis for the deduction that entropy changes are driven by probability. Provided that it is free to do so, anything will tend to move to a more probable state rather than a less probable one and the entropy change is directly related to this probability. The most probable state is also that which is the most disordered. In a disordered system there are quite simply far more ways of arranging the constituent parts than if we arrange them in a neat and ordered fashion. This makes the disordered state far more probable.

As an example of this principle that spontaneous events are driven by probability, we could take the example of sugar dissolved in a hot drink. If a spoonful of sugar is placed in a cup of hot tea or coffee then it will eventually dissolve and be spread throughout the cup, a process which can be speeded up by stirring the drink with a spoon. We know from experience that once the sugar has been dissolved in this way that it will not re-concentrate itself in one corner of the cup unless we dissolve an excessive amount of sugar and then cool the drink down. The reason why this re-concentration does not occur is that the even distribution of sugar throughout the tea or coffee after the sugar has dissolved has a far higher probability than does the situation where the sugar molecules have collected together in one place. Indeed, the possibility of such a collection occurring is so remote that we can say that it would never occur. From our knowledge of entropy it should be clear that sugar dissolved throughout the cup is also far more disordered than if it was all concentrated into one place. It is readily apparent that the entropy of such a system is closely related to its probability of occurring.

Further studies reveal that it is actually possible to calculate the entropy of a system by considering the number of different ways in which it is possible to arrange the molecules of which it is composed. These calculations involve very large numbers indeed which is why the natural processes which we observe around us are often so much more probable than any other eventual possibility that it is a virtual certainty that they will always occur.[6]

Calculations of the probability of how molecules will arrange themselves are known as statistical mechanics, which is an important branch of physical chemistry. Such studies provide the mathematical basis for the discussion so far. They demonstrate the way in which the effects of the increasing entropy or disorder which we see all around us have a sound predictable basis rather than being an observation which could conceivably find its explanation somewhere else. Our understanding of thermodynamics and statistical mechanics is well established and predates the advances in nuclear physics and cosmology which occurred during the twentieth century. Any good textbook on physical chemistry can be consulted for further details.

3.2 Entropy and Sin

At a superficial level, our description of entropy and the Second Law of Thermodynamics seems to resemble the doctrine of Original Sin. The Second Law describes the way in which the disorder of the universe is always increasing and how a spontaneous change can never be made to yield the maximum amount of work which is theoretically possible. The doctrine of Original Sin informs us that human nature is imperfect, in that we are never able to always behave in a manner which conforms to a given set of ethical principles, whatever these principles might be. Spontaneous natural processes can never yield the maximum amount of work and human nature can never behave in a way which is perfect. In both cases, effort and energy become directed elsewhere and events which are undesirable and unwanted will occur. If we take them to their ultimate conclusions, then within their own disciplines, both the Second Law of Thermodynamics and the doctrine of Original Sin provide a rationale for the death and decay which occur in the universe and for the observation that perfection is not possible. This failure to achieve perfection applies both to the field of human endeavor and also to the production of material objects.

This analysis seems to suggest that the apparent parallel between entropy and Sin may occur at two separate levels. It can certainly be seen in their effects, which could simply be a coincidence, but it might also be present in their causes, with the possibility that both the Second Law of Thermodynamics and the doctrine of Original Sin are the different ways in which two different disciplines describe the same basic phenomenon. It is possible that moral and physical disorder may have the same underlying cause.

However, when we consider its moral implications, this simple parallel appears to break down. Although we are used to thinking of Sin as being wrong, so that the doctrine of Original Sin makes a moral statement about the human race, there is no reason why we should apply the same description to the Second Law of Thermodynamics. The Second Law simply furnishes us with a morally neutral description of the universe and the way in which it operates, even if it does appear to be a flaw in the universe when viewed from the human perspective of a sentient and mortal life-form. Yet this apparent disagreement is likely to be nothing of the sort and occurs for a number of reasons. It could be caused by our confusion between Sin itself and sins, a confusion between cause and effect, which is effectively the distinction between the propensity to commit moral misdeeds and the deeds themselves. Alternatively, it could occur because we are unused to making ethical statements about pure science, or it could be that we have forgotten our own classifications. A statement about moral disorder will clearly have moral implications, whereas it could be argued that there is no necessary requirement for a statement about physical disorder to do the same.

If we first consider effects, then it is clear that sins, considered as moral misdeeds, are undesirable. By its very definition a sin is an action which is morally wrong, even if there is no complete unanimity as to which actions fall into this category. However, the reason that these actions are often thought of as being wrong is because they have consequences which are seen as being undesirable – an example of teleological ethics rather than absolute deontology, albeit that a deontological element is also present. In theological terms they are seen as the outcome of Sin (Original Sin); that state of existence in which we all inevitably make mistakes or do wrong. If we turn instead to the Second Law of Thermodynamics, then it is true that many of the consequences of this law are also undesirable. For example, it would be far better if heat engines such as power stations and car engines were 100 percent efficient. This would reduce pollution very significantly, both improving air quality and lessening climate change, as well as alleviating the world energy crisis. In their effects, there is a parallel between the Second Law and Original Sin. They both have undesirable consequences, a fact which could be pure coincidence or which could be describing something more fundamental about their relationship with each other.

When we turn our attention to causes, then the Second Law is usually thought of as being morally neutral. It is a statement of fact that any system is free to move to its most probable state of existence. In this sense it is important to note that the doctrine of Original Sin itself (as distinct from sins or misdeeds) is also morally neutral, in that it makes a statement about the freedom which is present in human nature – a freedom which allows us to do what is wrong as well as what is right. This is a radical statement to make, for we are not used to thinking of Sin as morally neutral. The problem with such an understanding is that Sin is an unfortunate word because it brings with itself a particular set of connotations. It is true that the account of events in the Garden of Eden places a morally wrong action at the basis of the doctrine, but this is no more than an illustration of human nature. The doctrine of Original Sin makes a statement about the way in which human beings will behave, in the same way as the Second Law of Thermodynamics makes a statement about the way in which the universe will behave. Just as there are people who refuse to accept that human nature is 'fallen' in this way and believe that we can tend towards perfection if we could try hard enough, so there are people who delude themselves into thinking that the ageing process need not be inevitable or that it is possible to produce perpetual motion, and that in one of these ways they can beat the Second Law.

When we describe the Second Law and Original Sin in this way, then from the human perspective they can both seem to be inherent flaws in the universe and neither of them can be blamed on any living person. People may die as a result and natural disasters will occur, but in generic terms, these two sets of observations are not our fault and we have no control over them. It is, of course, true that the effects of entropy can be overcome on a local basis and that it is possible to move chemical systems to a state in which they are more ordered, but this can only be achieved by the input of energy and the concomitant increase in entropy elsewhere. This parallels the way in which strenuous effort or moral revulsion can produce a short-term conquest of local evil which can never apply universally, whether it be to all people in all places or to the whole life of a particular individual. This inevitability does not remove the blame which is attached to immoral actions; it is simply to make the observation that some immorality is bound to occur somewhere. Both an increase in Sin and an increase in entropy can apparently be overcome but only locally and only at a considerable cost.

When we were considering entropy (or disorder) in section 3.1, we noted that states which have a greater entropy are more probable than states with a lower entropy. There is nothing remarkable about this statement as it is simply an outcome of fairly basic statistics. It therefore seems logical to ask whether this same effect applies to Sin. Is a state with a higher level of Sin more probable than one which has less? However, this question misses the point that the parallel exists (or seems to exist) between Sin and the Second Law itself, so that entropy would find its parallel with moral misdemeanors. As a result, if we enquire as to the possible parallels which may exist to the increase in entropy with time, the conclusion has to be that this does not reside in the total number of moral misdemeanors occurring per hour or per day, but in the total number ever committed. Our reaction to this statement should be to observe that it is self-evident. The total number of moral misdemeanors committed can never decrease, unless we reverse time. However, the same is true of entropy – it too can never decrease when taken as a whole; it is just that we are not used to thinking about entropy and so this is less self-evident. The parallel to a local region of order will be a place or time in which few moral misdemeanors occur and in which the effect of these on the wider world is minimized. Neither of these effects can be sustained indefinitely.

At a deeper level, this debate is tied in with the concept of freedom. Human sins are possible because we have freedom of action, in that our behavior is not prescribed for us and we have a choice in the way in which we act. It is a more or less universal observation that moral misdeeds are the inevitable outcome of such freedom. Entropy is also about freedom, in that systems are free to adopt their most probable configuration and are therefore driven by their own internal workings towards their natural end. Both the occurrence of moral misdemeanors or sins and the increase in overall entropy are the result of freedom.

The doctrine of Original Sin describes the moral consequences of freedom and attempts to explain these in theological terms. The Second Law of Thermodynamics describes the molecular consequences of freedom, together with their macroscopic manifestations, and explains them in scientific terms. It is a fundamental observation that neither the law nor the doctrine can be overcome in the universe as we know it. However, in a book about theology, we have to ask whether this universe is all that there is and how our understanding of God impinges on these observations. In particular we have to ask what the doctrines of salvation and re-creation might have to say not only about overcoming Sin but also about the conquest of entropy. The entropy of the universe can only decrease if there is an input of order from beyond the universe. It can be argued that the same applies to moral misdemeanors and that their annulment is called forgiveness – absolute forgiveness. This importance of forgiveness implies that the doctrine of the atonement is crucial to this whole discussion. This is the subject we shall discuss in Chapter 4. In both of these cases the problem revolves around freedom and the way in which this is influenced by time.

3.3 Time and Freedom

It appears from our discussions so far that both Original Sin and the Second Law of Thermodynamics involve the concept of freedom and that they describe systems which are liable to change and which are open to the future. However, this discussion begs the question as to what might happen in a situation where entropy no longer increases with time. Theologically, we are used to talking about a situation beyond the present existence in which Sin is no longer a problem; a situation which is traditionally called 'heaven'. The issue now is to examine the consequences of such a situation for the behavior of entropy. If our parallel between Original Sin and the Second Law is to be meaningful, we must ask whether we can speak of the thermodynamic consequences of such a condition.

The Second Law of Thermodynamics describes the way in which entropy increases with time and we have come to understand that this process is linked to the freedom of action within the universe.[7] However, it is important to ask what happens to freedom if entropy no longer increases with time and what would then be the implications for the way in which we understand the concept of time itself. For the physical scientist, these are interesting but largely hypothetical questions. For the Christian theologian they are important because if our theology has to be consistent with the way the world is, then we need to consider the consequences for freedom, time and entropy if God should re-create the universe in accordance with traditional eschatological expectations. To put the question another way, if heaven is free of pain and decay, then what are the consequences for the Second Law of Thermodynamics and for freedom? This is an important question irrespective of whether this re-creation is seen as otherworldly or as a continuum with the present creation.

One possible solution to these questions lies within our understanding of time and the way in which time as we experience it in this world relates to time in the new creation. Time has to be understood as being a part of creation, so that the increase in entropy within time is concomitant with that time. It may be that within the new order of things, time does not work in quite the same way, so that the relationship between entropy and time is altered.

Russell Stannard has noted that although it is not possible to distinguish between the two directions on a given spatial axis (forwards and backwards, or right and left, both look the same, so that if we are only allowed to look in one direction then we do not know which it is) this is not true if we consider the time axis.[8] As an example, if we move the position of a cake within a kitchen, then the cake remains the same and looks the same wherever we place it. However, if we examine the same cake along the time axis, then the raw ingredients precede the finished cake – a simple example of applied chemistry and the increase of entropy with time. It is an example of one of those things which we learn in childhood and then take for granted. The appearance of the cake is not dependent on its position in space but it is dependent on its position in time.

However, it is important to realize that observations such as the changes which occur when a cake is baked or a glass vase is dropped onto a tiled floor do not actually imply that time flows, only that we perceive it as such. The finished cake and its ingredients exist at different points along the time axis, one of which we label as 'earlier' and another as 'later'. As we move along the axis in this direction, from earlier to later, so entropy increases. However, there is nothing in the laws of physics as we understand them at present which prohibits movement in the opposite direction – it is only that we never perceive time flowing backwards.

This same understanding of time scales and the flow of time appears in the physiology of the human body, and apparently occurs in the mind as well, although our recollections of past time are not always clear. It is undecided whether temporal directionality is necessary or only a feature of our experience. Stephen Hawking has argued that when information is stored, whether this is mentally, in biological structures, or otherwise, so energy must be expended. This has the consequence that part of this energy must be dissipated as heat which then produces a consequential increase in the overall disorder and entropy of the universe.[9] As a consequence, our subjective or mental time must run parallel to thermodynamic time and cosmic time. However, because the universe is expanding, the increasing disorder is spread over an increasing volume of space and is therefore not deleterious to the emergence of order on a local scale. Stephen

Hawking has also calculated that such an increase in entropy would also have to occur when information is stored in a contracting universe. The result of this is that intelligent life would not then be possible as a continually increasing amount of disorder would have to be contained within a continually decreasing amount of space.

The question which we now need to answer is what this discussion can usefully contribute to our understanding of God's new creation and whether this new creation can avoid the apparent flaw which we experience as natural disasters and human evil. If the discussion is only abstract, then its value is limited. From the theological perspective, the eschatological new creation is, of course, the consummation of our destiny as beings which are able to make manifest the God who created us. When we and the universe are re-created, we will be able to show forth God much better than we can at present. As such we might expect that in God's new creation we would still be able to enjoy freedom of action and decision, but that there would be an absence of both moral evil (the manifestations of Sin) and of natural evil – those natural events which we can attribute to an increase in the disorder of the universe.

According to St Augustine, true freedom lies in the ability not to sin (*posse non peccare*) rather than in the inability to sin (*non posse peccare*). As such, if we believe that freedom is good and is part of the will of God, then the Kingdom of God would be a place and time where sins were possible but never manifest, rather than a place and time where sin was impossible. This seems to imply that the inherent sinfulness which is present within human nature (Original Sin) would in some sense still be present, but that it would never receive expression in thought or deed. It is as if the perfect presence of the perfect love of God renders it inoperative. This may seem to be heretical, because it seems to imply that there is an imperfection in God's re-creation, but it is perfectly consistent with those descriptions of the

73

atonement (the way in which we are saved by the death of Christ), in which atonement works through God regarding us as if we were righteous or through our participation in Jesus Christ, but not with those in which we are made perfect.[10] It is also consistent with the moral argument which we considered earlier, namely that Sin itself (which now becomes a somewhat unfortunate term) is morally neutral – it is simply a statement about the freedom which has been given to the creation. It is the manifestation of Sin itself as actual sins or misdeeds which causes the moral problem.

What are the consequences of this for entropy? If freedom is present in this new creation and if entropy still increases as a result, how is natural evil and disorder to be averted? One solution is perhaps to observe that if we are thinking of God's new creation as being otherworldly, then it might exist beyond our current conception of time, so that if there is no movement in time, then there is no necessary increase in entropy. Perhaps this is akin to suggesting that Original Sin is still about, but that it cannot find expression. However, if the Kingdom of God is in some way a continuation of the present world, then this is more problematical. There is the clear implication that freedom is removed and that God is therefore no longer creative. The alternative is to work on the premise that the universe is not a closed system from the standpoint of God. If God can act beyond the universe as well as within it, then a suitable energy transfer can occur which results in an internal decrease in entropy without removing freedom and creativity.

The above arguments are, of course, speculation. They are included here not because they are necessarily correct, for we have no way of knowing how much truth they contain, but because they demonstrate the point that a dialogue between science and Christian thought is possible within our framework. These are the sorts of issues which arise from the discussion as to whether the doctrine of Original Sin and the Second Law of

Thermodynamics might actually be opposite sides of the same coin. We are traveling through uncharted territory. Indeed, if we wanted to speculate further, it might be that reductionism – that idea that everything can be calculated from basic information such as the properties of subatomic particles – is not possible because of the universal increase in entropy which we know as the Second Law of Thermodynamics. The disorder which is caused by the storage and computation of the colossal amount of information involved outweighs the order which accrues due to the product of the predictive process. It would be ironic if reductionism could be possible only in a situation where there is no increase in entropy. It is possible that both theologically and scientifically, the only place where the dream of being able to calculate everything from first principles could be true is in the Kingdom of God!

However, this whole discussion begs the question that if the fall can be reversed in this manner, then why was this new world not created to begin with? There is no obvious answer to the question. The best answer is, perhaps, something to do with memory. It could be that the new existence (heaven or whatever it happens to be called) would itself beg questions if it were not for the memory that we would continue to hold of our time in this world of freedom and Original Sin, where disorder is continually on the increase. Without this memory of the present world, the new world would not make sense. Perhaps, to borrow the language of St Paul, we shall only be able to see clearly and face to face because we have first of all seen in a glass darkly or because we have seen the puzzle which is presented by our present life.

3.4 The Worldview
If the ideas which we have discussed in the previous sections are to be helpful and are to inform us about the relationship between science and the Christian faith, then they must be able to relate

to and be coherent with the Christian worldview which we discussed in Chapter 1. According to this view there are four principles which underlie Christian theology. The first of these is that it tells a coherent story, the second that it provides answers to the four questions of existence (namely 'Who are we?', 'Where are we?', 'What is wrong?' and 'What is the solution?'), the third that it finds expression in symbolic artefacts, and the fourth that it gives rise to a particular way of living in the world. We shall consider each of these four principles in turn and then make a few comments based on our discussion so far.

Taking first the Christian story, it should be clear from our exploration, that the Second Law of Thermodynamics is consistent with the content of the Christian narratives in that its content and consequences contain nothing which need contradict the central premises of the Christian faith. Indeed, it could be argued that through its themes of freedom and disorder, the Second Law parallels quite neatly the human story of rebellion and waywardness which characterize the behavior of God's people through the millennia, both before and after Christ. The Christian story and the Old Testament description of the people of Israel provide accounts of God's people, and the Second Law of Thermodynamics is a description of the world in which they live and move.

The four questions of existence bring us closer to the crux of the matter. In Chapter 1, we have already seen that Wright answers the first question, namely that of our identity, by stating that we are human beings made in the image of our creator. A consequence of this is that we ourselves are creative and that as a result we tend to work against the decay which we experience in the world. We now know that the way in which this decay occurs can be described by the Second Law of Thermodynamics. The second question, namely that of our location, was answered in terms of a beautiful but transient world – transient, we now discover, because of the inbuilt factors described by that Second

Law.

The third question, which concerns the nature of the problem, was answered by Wright in theological terms through the account of a rebellion against the creator. Wright noted that this reflects a cosmic dislocation which exists between the creator and the creation – what we are calling a 'flaw' in the universe. In our terms, this dislocation could be identified with the Second Law, although this then begs the question as to how the dislocation came to be present in the first place. Human creativity is inevitably dislocated since we work with materials subject to the Second Law. The divine creation, of which we are a part, includes this law, unless we are to suppose that it was planted by some outside agency traditionally described in terms of the devil or Satan. The answer has to be that the Second Law of Thermodynamics is a part of creation in that it is an expression of freedom, something which in itself is good, but that it is also accompanied by consequences which anything experiencing that freedom has to accept. In a sense, this is a part of the Christian story in that in the Garden of Eden, Adam and Eve were implicitly allowed to eat from the tree of life but forbidden to eat from the tree of the knowledge of good and evil. Their choice of good and evil is a statement of the way the world is. The story was produced in the early days of our religious heritage to explain human mortality.[11] This attempt to rationalize the way the world is, can clearly be understood as an attempt to rationalize the consequences of what we now know as the Second Law of Thermodynamics. A world which is based on freedom is a world in which things can and do go wrong through the increase of disorder.

The final of the four questions, namely that of the solution, is answered by Wright in terms of the creator entering His creation in order to deal with the human rebellion and to bring it to the end for which it was made. In our scheme of things, we have to find the solution to the question not of human rebellion but rather of the cosmic dislocation or flaw in the universe. The simple answer lies in the significance of the actions of Christ for the whole cosmos and not merely for life on earth. The more complex answer lies in the way in which the Second Law would be superseded in a new creation, a subject which we have discussed in section 3.3.

At this point, however, we need to be cautious. In adopting this approach and arguing that a new creation would annul the Second Law of Thermodynamics it could seem that science is being made subservient to theology. This is not the case. The Second Law is part of the universe as we experience it; a universe which theology refers to as the 'creation'. If a Christian is to talk about the renewal of the creation, then the Second Law is a part of that creation which is to be renewed and he or she has to try and explain how a new creation without such a law is possible when it was an apparent necessity in the first place. Science is about describing and understanding the universe as it is and theology has had continually to restate its fundamental truths in a language which is consistent with our changes in scientific understanding. Theology has to accept the results of a genuine quest for knowledge in all other fields of human endeavor. However, it is no great obstacle for science, nor is it being made subservient to theology, if it is asked to consider the 'What if?' of re-creation, especially as science fiction poses similar sorts of questions on a regular basis.

When we move on to Wright's third principle, namely the interaction with Christian artefacts and symbols, then we find a much more limited application to the present discussion. Yet even here, the principal Christian symbol, namely the cross, is as much a statement of God's response to disorder and decay as it is to Original Sin and to sins. On the cross, God takes to Himself the unsatisfactory consequences of living in the world which He has created, including the pain and suffering as well as death. In theological terms, God can only truly forgive if the misdeed has been directed against Him. The death of Christ is a sin of humanity, but the death itself is made possible by the way the world is.

Chapter 1 ended with the claim that the Christian way of being in the world was where we should find the outworkings of the Christian response to the Second Law and, in particular, the interaction of this law with the Christian gospel. So far, we have only come a short part of the way down this road. We still need to get to grips with the wider implications of our basic premise. In the next chapter we shall focus on the atonement, an area where a discussion of the relationship should prove very fruitful, since this is where the Christian faith deals with the issues related to sin, suffering and death. Indeed, suffering is an important issue which is often on the lips of people as they question the nature of their existence. If our exploration can enable us to say something about suffering and natural evil then we shall have made an important contribution to theological debate and its relevance to daily life.

However, we must not stop at the atonement. We also need to relate our findings to the other major themes of Christian doctrine, such as the Trinity and Christology. Christology and the Trinity are vital elements of the ways in which we understand God and describe God. Taken together, they form the Christian doctrine of God, but even then they are not the complete story. The doctrine of the resurrection is also fundamental to Christian faith and belief as well as to our understanding of the Divinity, as is the study of creation. They are important not only in a pure theological sense but also because they inform our worship. These areas will occupy our attention throughout Chapter 5 as we consider the doctrines of God, resurrection and creation.

Finally, we need to look forwards and to ask what further implications this discussion might have as well as exploring the questions which it has posed and left unanswered. At the heart of this discussion lies the interplay which exists between experience and faith, together with the ways in which these both inform our theological thinking and our scientific endeavors. It is the dialogue which offers the greatest scope for asking the real questions and for beginning to find the answers which inform and nourish those who care to seek them out.

4

Atonement and the Second Law

The cross stands right at the heart of the Christian faith. It is both the place and the means of the death of Jesus Christ and it has become the widely accepted symbol for Christianity. The empty cross is a sign of hope through its reminder of the resurrection, whilst the crucifix, in which the body hangs in death on the cross, is a reminder of God's great love for us and of His gift of Himself to us. The sixteenth-century German reformer Philip Melanchthon noted that 'Who Jesus Christ is becomes known in his saving action', implying that it is on the cross that the true nature of Jesus is revealed.[1] As Jürgen Moltmann put it, 'In Christianity the cross is the test of everything which deserves to be called Christian. One may add that the cross alone, and nothing else, is its test...'[2] We cannot overemphasize the power of the cross as an inspiration to both faith and action and its importance in Christian doctrine, unless in so doing we play down or exclude other essential or core elements of the Christian faith.

The above claim made by Moltmann is important, not least because if he is correct then it is in the cross that we should find the answers to the difficult questions which are asked of the Christian faith and which it needs to be seen to address if it is to be credible in the present day. Questions such as why people suffer through accident or violence, why we have to die and why natural disasters occur are asked repeatedly by a great many people, and any religious faith which wants to be taken seriously needs to be able to answer them in an understandable and satisfactory manner. The centrality of the cross also implies that the interplay with scientific thought which occurs in our theological understanding of the cross will be vital to any serious understanding of the relationship between science and theology.

Throughout this chapter, the key theme is that of the atonement – the question of how we can be reconciled to and made at one with God. The importance of Jesus' death and the understanding of the atonement was one of the key issues which drove the early church to work out its understanding of the person of Christ (Christology), and the subject remains crucial to the Christian faith in the present day. We shall explore the question of how far we can extend this understanding as we seek to relate the Christian faith beyond its own worldview and into that of science.

4.1 Theories of the Atonement

The word 'atonement' literally means the process through which two parties who used to be estranged from each other in some way have now become 'at one' and reconciled to each other. In Christian theology it is used to refer to the restoration of the damaged relationship between God and humanity through the crucifixion of Jesus Christ. The other key words to note here are 'righteousness' and 'justification', both of which are used in translating Greek words with the root δικαιοσ (*dikaios*), a concept which implies that the parties involved are now part of a right relationship or doing justice to the relationship in which they stand. However, there has always been a great deal of debate about how this restored relationship was achieved and how we are made at one with God. Throughout the history of the church a great many theories have been developed to explain this restoration of relationship.[3] Such theories cover a wide spectrum of Christian beliefs and each of them tells us a great deal about the theological understanding of its proponents. In the present day they can be used almost as a measure of the theological stance of a given individual Christian.

The various theories of the atonement also use a wide variety of language. Some of them describe Christ as gaining a victory over sin and death through His crucifixion and resurrection, a victory in which we share and in which we can participate through our faith, whilst others envisage a change in our legal status through Christ's obedience to the cross. This changed legal status is akin to an acquittal and thereby gives rise to the language of justification, since we are justified before God. Other images in use include that of liberation, in which we are released from the imprisonment of sin and death, and that of wholeness, in which Christ makes us whole and restores us to health. Several of these ideas lead to the concept of salvation, since they share the claim that we are saved from something.

The earliest recorded Christian ideas which we possess on the atonement are those of St Paul. His conclusions, based on his understanding of Sin and death, have colored Christian theology ever since. However, it is important to realize that Paul did not have just one theory of the atonement but that he made use of many different models – a fact which is often ignored. This is an important lesson for those Christians who like everything in their faith to be neat and tidy and who believe that the atonement has to be understood in a single particular way if they are to avoid the risk of compromising their Christian faith.

As examples of St Paul's ideas, we could note that in chapter 15 verse 3 of his first letter to the Corinthians he wrote that 'Christ died for our sins' and that in chapter 5 verses 17–19 of the second letter to the Corinthians he expanded this theme by writing that 'in Christ God was reconciling the world to himself' and that anyone who is in Christ is a 'new creation'. In his letter to the Romans the ideas as to how this was achieved come thick and fast: chapter 3 verses 23–26 contain the ideas of redemption, expiation or propitiation and the blood of Christ. The concept of redemption suggests that there was a price to be paid for our freedom, expiation that our status was changed, and propitiation that the wrath of God needed to be satisfied. The blood of Christ quite obviously speaks of His death. It is interesting to note the variety of translations which can be found for the key words which are present in verse 25. Here, the Greek word ηιλαστεριον (*hilasterion* – literally 'mercy seat', the place of sacrifice in the temple) is variously translated as 'expiation', 'propitiation', 'sacrificial death' or 'sacrifice of atonement'. The exact wording tells us more about the theology of the translator than that of St Paul. Romans chapter 5 verses 6–11 make it clear that Paul was happy to make use of the idea of appeasing the wrath of God, whilst chapter 6 verses 3–8 move the argument away from Sin to a consideration of death and new life following a sharing in a resurrection like that of Christ.

The important point about these writings of St Paul is that he used a variety of images and language and that therefore he was unlikely to have felt that there was one correct explanation – or at least that such an explanation was unavailable to human thought. It is likely that he used a multiplicity of images in order to attempt and explore something which defied a simple explanation in this way. The mystery of God's saving grace is far too profound for a simple and facile human explanation. We should also recall that Paul came to this debate from a different direction to the way in which the Christian church has usually approached the issue. As a devout Jew, Saul – as he was then known – would not have felt that he needed to be saved. His experience on the Damascus road, when he had a quite literally blinding vision of the risen Christ, asking him why he was persecuting Him, changed this view of life. It became clear to him that he needed the salvation which was to be found in Jesus Christ, but he also needed to answer the question as to what it was that he needed salvation from and why this was necessary.

The church, on the other hand, has usually presumed that we all know that we commit immoral actions and that these are a problem which weighs us down. The church then presents salvation in Jesus Christ as the solution to our problem. The problems and the consequences of physical evil and human questions about death and suffering are usually ignored, despite the fact that for many people these are far more vital issues than their own immorality. It might be both helpful and healthy if Christian teaching recognized both Paul's own personal perspective as well as the priorities embodied in the questions which occur in our daily life. These questions of death and suffering are not a separate secular issue which deflect us from the presentation of the gospel, but rather a different set of questions to which the central good news of the Christian faith still provides the answer.

The one constant strand in all of Paul's ideas is that Paul believed that something had been done *for* us: there was an external agent at work. However, it is important to remember that this view is not universal within the Christian faith. When people explain how they understand the atonement, their ideas or theories usually fall into one of two general categories. These are known as subjective and objective theories of the atonement, and it is only in the latter that we find the idea that something has been done for us.

In the subjective view of the atonement, it is believed that Christ died as an example, and that His death changes the attitude of those who respond to this example. In other words, we undergo a change of heart when we see Christ crucified. This view was championed by Peter Abelard (1079–1142) but condemned by most other Christian writers of the time. It has grown in popularity over the past two hundred years and is now promoted by many writers whose theological position could generally be described as 'liberal'. Its growing popularity is undoubtedly linked to the rise in individualism within Western society and the feeling that we need to be self-reliant and able to do things for ourselves. It also fits neatly with the fact that we do not like to be wrong. The subjective view of the atonement suggests that we could be perfect if only we would be sufficiently inspired to try hard enough.

Despite its recent popularity there are a number of important objections to the subjective view of the atonement. The first objection is that it relies upon our restoring our relationship with God by our own efforts. If we follow traditional Christian doctrine then this view is undoubtedly heretical as it is a form of Pelagianism (see below). However, more telling is the practical observation that if it were possible for us to restore our relationship in this way, then there would have been no need for Christ to die at all – we could just have got on with it ourselves. The second objection is that the theory fails to answer Anselm's question, 'Cur Deus Homo? (Why did God become Man?)' If the atonement is achieved purely by the example of someone dying, then why was it necessary for God Himself to become incarnate rather than our being inspired by the death of a good man?

In response to these objections, some holders of the subjective view would argue that in order for the example which we have been set to be effective and to inspire us to change our ways, then it had to be an example set by God Himself in which He showed how much He loves us. Only God Himself could evoke sufficient response in human hearts. A stronger response to these objections to the subjective view would simply reject the first objection out of hand, claiming that we can indeed restore this relationship ourselves, and address only the second objection. This can then be dismissed on the grounds that Jesus Christ was not divine, that He was simply a good man, and so this change of heart was indeed achieved by the example of a good person. It would be claimed that there is no need to answer Anselm's question, on the grounds that it is invalid because God did not actually become human.

The sad fact is that such subjective understandings of the atonement constitute a 'no-hope' theology in that it is quite clear from looking at the world around us that no-one has ever succeeded in living a perfect life and thereby demonstrated that the subjective approach can work. Indeed – and this is the underlying premise behind this book – I would argue that there is an innate Sinfulness about human nature and that something similar seems to apply to the world at large. There is an apparent flaw in the universe and one of the consequences of this flaw is that nothing can ever be perfect. Although we can be inspired to great efforts by the death of Christ, ultimately we will fail to live perfectly good lives. The whole idea that we can be good by our own will can only produce a sense of guilt and failure as we repeatedly fail in our attempt and come to realize that there is no hope of ever being able to satisfy its demands. To claim that we can live a perfect life may seem to be taking an optimistic approach, but it is doomed to repeated failure and increasing despair. To acknowledge the fallen state of the universe may seem pessimistic, but it allows for the hope which is to be found in Jesus Christ.

This whole question of whether it is possible to live a life without sinning was one of the major theological controversies at the beginning of the fifth century. The argument concerned the difference in belief between Augustine of Hippo (354–430), who was undoubtedly the greatest Christian thinker of his day, and the followers of Pelagius (d. c.410) who was a monk, probably of Irish origin. It is worth noting that Pelagius himself was probably rather more moderate than the heretical belief which is described by his name and that Augustine's real dispute lay with his followers, albeit that most of the blame has always been laid on Pelagius himself.

The debate between the followers of Augustine and Pelagius was complex and acrimonious. However, the argument centered upon the question as to whether the freedom which is enjoyed by human beings makes it possible to live a life without sinning (*posse non peccare*). Augustine believed that this was impossible, a view undoubtedly influenced by his own earlier life and the tensions which he still felt within himself. The Pelagian position was that it was possible. The followers of Pelagius would be able to point to the way in which Pelagius had transformed the morals of a large number of the Roman young people of his day.

In short, Augustine won the battle and Pelagius was condemned by the church, although not by Augustine who only disagreed with the views which were reported to him. It is worth noting that leading patristic scholars now claim that both men have been widely misunderstood and are repeatedly misrepresented by many popular Christian writers in the present day. However, it is still true that if the followers of Pelagius were right then the subjective view of the atonement could be valid. If Augustine was right then the subjective view of the atonement is a 'no-hope' theology.[4]

If we move our attention to the objective view of the atonement, we should first note that this is the belief that Christ actually did something for us and that we are incapable of restoring our relationship with God by our own efforts. This has generally been the mainstream Christian position and was championed by Anselm (1033–1109), the then Archbishop of Canterbury. His writings on the subject were the most influential since those produced during the first few centuries of the church and the title of his book *Cur Deus Homo* is still widely used. In his writing, Anselm not only endeavored to explain the atonement but also meditated on the incarnation and tried to play down the medieval overemphasis on Christ as judge. This was important, because if the savior is portrayed as a cruel judge then humanity will seek an alternative savior. Within the Christian faith, both a harsh god and a god who is irrelevant will lead to similar attributes of cruelty or irrelevance being ascribed to the church. Neither of these views is particularly helpful and at various times they have both led to a rejection of the Christian church.

Although the objective view has long been the mainstream Christian tradition, it is by no means a homogeneous set of beliefs. There are a wide variety of views of the atonement which can be described as objective and each writer on the subject seems to add his or her own nuance. The discussion below focuses on the three principal positions, but we should recall that other variations are possible and that many are much more involved than space here allows. However, they all share the common theme that Christ actually did something for us in His death and that He was not simply an example to us.

The first principal objective position is substitutionary atonement. This is the view that when Christ died on the cross, He died in our place instead of us. He died the death which we deserved because we have disobeyed God. This could be called the 'traditional' view. There can be little doubt that this was the general position which covered the range of ideas voiced by St Paul and there are many images which are used to illustrate this idea, such as 'ransom' and 'buying' or 'purchase'. However, there is also an important distinction to be made between two competing ideas of substitutionary atonement. This distinction has caused heated debate within evangelical theology, most notably on how to translate chapter 3 verse five of Paul's letter to the Romans. This is the distinction which is made between expiation and propitiation.

Expiation is the view that when Christ died in our place, He changed our status because He paid the price for our sins. We are no longer estranged from God because the price has now been paid. Propitiation, on the other hand, is the view that when Christ died in our place, He changed God's attitude towards us by appeasing the wrath of God. The idea is that because God is good then He is justly angry with anyone who sins. This anger is sometimes termed the 'wrath of God'. However, because this is righteous anger, God cannot simply forgive us as in imputed atonement (see below), nor is it satisfactory for someone to voluntarily die in our place to pay the price and thereby change our status as in expiation. Neither of these could actually satisfy the righteous wrath of God which has to be appeased by punishing the actual person who has committed the misdeed or someone who does not deserve to be punished but who is never-theless prepared to take their place. The only person who fits the latter description is Jesus and so He is punished in our place.[5]

Despite its popularity in evangelical theology, many people view propitiation with distaste since it seems to paint a picture which describes a vindictive God, who takes it all out on Jesus. This view fails to take account of the righteousness which is attached to God's anger and the fact that since Jesus is actually one of the three persons of the divine Trinity, then God is, in a sense, taking the anger out on Himself. Nevertheless, perhaps the strongest argument against propitiation is that the theory is too neat and tidy. It implies that we can fully understand the actions of Christ on the cross as well as God's redeeming love. It is a theory which removes the mystery from religion.

The second of the three principal objective positions on the atonement is that of imputed (or fictitious) atonement, often referred to as 'forensic justification'.[6] Forensic justification was developed at the time of the Reformation by Philip Melanchthon, working with ideas put forward by Martin Luther. In this scheme of things, God forgives us for our sins and imputes righteousness to us. Rather than actually being made righteous, God reckons His own righteousness (that of Christ) as if it were a part of us. It is as if we are pronounced to be righteous by decision of God and to be counted as righteous, even though God knows that we are guilty and that we will accrue further guilt in the future. In this scheme of things, righteousness is like a garment which is put on and which can cover up all manner of things underneath. These ideas are sometimes referred to as 'fictitious' atonement because the Sin has not been removed nor human nature changed; it is simply that we have been declared as righteous. According to Melanchthon, the process of being made righteous was a separate and subsequent step. A critic might say that this theory suggests that Jesus has rigged the judicial process in our favor, although this observation perhaps misses the point that legal metaphors may not necessarily be the most helpful way of discussing something which stems from God's love and that Melanchthon might have been wiser to have avoided them.

The third principal objective position is sometimes called the 'classical view', a term introduced by the Swedish theologian Gustav Aulen (1879–1977) and presented in his book *Christus Victor*.[7] In this view, Aulen sees atonement operating through our participation in the death of Christ and in our anticipated participation in His resurrection. In this view Christ died vicariously, on our behalf, but has emerged victorious over death, defeating the powers of evil – hence the term 'Christus Victor'. In his work, Aulen showed that this was the view which was most widely held within the early church and which was described by its principal theological writers. It had been largely overlooked in more recent times because it was often presented in language which implied some sort of transaction with Satan and which was therefore felt to be distasteful.

In fact, the wide variety of language which the early writers used suggests that they generally held this 'classical view' but were unsure of how to describe it in precise terms. Indeed, Aulen makes the point that unlike the other positions which we have discussed above, this is not a developed theory but rather a general view. The important point in these classical descriptions was the participation which was involved whereby anyone who is baptized participates in the death of Christ and in so doing receives the promise that they will also participate in His resurrection. This idea can also be found in the writings of St Paul, being present in chapter 6 of his letter to the Romans. Aulen actually goes as far as to separate this 'classical view' from the objective theories, since it is not actually a theory. He claims that it is rather the earliest view and the one from which the theories grew. We should take note that this idea of participation is crucial to our present argument because it shifts the focus away from sins and towards death. In pursuing the theme of our book, too much emphasis on morals is not helpful and we should be more interested in the status of humanity in the eyes of God, and the way in which this links with the twin themes of death and suffering.

4.2 Death and Suffering

The various theories of the atonement provide a range of methods for addressing the problem of human guilt and the question of how sinful humanity can be reconciled to God. They were developed primarily to address the issue of Sin or sins and either the needs of a society which demanded a solution to the problems of Sin, or those of individuals (like Saul on the Damascus road) who had been convinced that they needed a solution – that they needed to be saved. However, when we take the care to look, it is clear that many of the theories of the atonement are not so satisfactory in addressing the questions which are posed by death and suffering, those questions which are far more on the minds of people in the present day.

The theological challenge of providing a satisfactory explanation of how the God of love can allow suffering in the world is perennial and the development of what is known as 'theodicy' has long challenged theologians. In the present context, we might want to argue that given the close connection between Sin and death, if a theory of the atonement can also address the issues involved with theodicy, then it is much more believable than a theory which cannot achieve this.

Death can be understood as part of the human condition – an event which we must all face – and which is answered by the promise that all who are baptized into the death of Jesus Christ will also share in His resurrection, even if this then begs the question as to the fate of those who are not baptized. Suffering, on the other hand, defies explanation in this scheme of things. One common idea, namely that human suffering is a punishment for our misdeeds, simply will not do within the context of the atonement because such punishment has already been dealt with by the death of Christ on the cross. This idea of suffering as punishment also fails to take account of suffering in the non-human world. An alternative explanation which is also common within popular theology, namely that God wills suffering in order to help us to grow, is also wholly unsatisfactory. We must be absolutely clear that God does not will any form of suffering upon His creation. Suffering occurs because of the way the world has to be, or to put it another way, suffering is inevitable. When suffering is viewed from the perspective of wanting a trouble-free existence it is the universal flaw in creation. Suffering may well contribute to the development of character, but it will not do to claim that the God who is described as 'Love' wills suffering on His creation for its own good, even if His ultimate will is to redeem the whole creation and not merely the human race.

This whole issue of theodicy troubles many Christians and is a perennial theological problem, not least for those who feel that Christ defeated the powers of evil on the cross and that bad things should not happen to His followers. Although Christians and indeed deists sometimes infer the existence of God from the beauty of the universe, proponents of atheism also draw evidence for their position from the existence of the world and from the everyday experiences of men and women. They find no conclusive evidence for the presence of the God of Love in that world. Indeed, through the observation of human suffering, they claim rather to find the opposite and thereby produce evidence for their disbelief.[8]

Rowan Williams has noted that the key to solving this problem of suffering is the language of the Christus Victor tradition or the classical view of the atonement. Rather than implying or claiming that the atonement has brought order to the world, this approach takes the problems of the world seriously. These problems have not been obliterated but are rather in the process of being overcome. They are still present with us in the world, but their traumas are to be seen not only for what they are, but also as the prints of the nails in the body of Jesus Christ. His resurrection is the demonstration and promise that they will never be the ultimate victors but that God will ultimately triumph.[9] In writing this, Williams echoes St Paul, again writing in his letter to the Romans, when he notes that 'the creation itself will be set free from its bondage to decay and will obtain the freedom of the glory of the children of God'.[10]

It may be that the overwhelming and damaging obsession with sins which has preoccupied both the church and a great many of its members since the Middle Ages has too often led theologians to ignore the fact that the above emphasis on suffering and death is also present in the writings of the patristic era. As an example, Athanasius saw death as an ever-present threat to the order which is present in God's creation and he taught that the Word of God worked to remove the consequences of this threat. Although the death and suffering was closely tied up with Sin, it was still an important element of his teaching. Alvyn Pettersen has noted that it is important not to underestimate the degree to which Athanasius understood death in this way.[11]

Athanasius' view on the significance of death was linked to his strong views on creation and the order which had been wrought by the Word of God – an order which was threatened by the disorder of death. However, this threat was not to be understood as a separate issue to that of Sin. Athanasius was thoroughly Pauline in such matters, seeing death as the consequence of people turning away from God and towards unwholesome desires. For Athanasius, death was the result of alienation from God, who is the source of all being and whose Word created us from nothingness. Whilst Athanasius does deal with Sin and fallen human nature, he also sees the practical importance of relating this to the issue of death. It is also important to note that Athanasius understood that the whole of creation has a fallen nature and that the salvation wrought by the Word of God applies to this whole creation and not only to humanity. In this view, Athanasius again followed Paul, as is clear from a reading of Romans chapter 8 verses 22–23. The issue of death and suffering is one which affects the whole universe and not simply the human race. By implication, natural disasters form a part of the scheme of things which are to be redeemed in Christ.

A similar point was made in medieval times by Hugh of St Victor. If the whole of the created order is to be understood as the work of the Word of God, then any restoration wrought by Christ must similarly apply to the whole of this created order. The whole creation is fallen but the whole creation also shares in the redemption of Jesus Christ and hence in the resurrection of the body.[12] The point is often made that although Jesus was a man, it was His humanity, rather than His masculine gender, which was important as far as salvation is concerned. It may be the case that the really important point is that although He was 'begotten not made', He nevertheless was composed of the same matter as the creation in order to redeem that creation. The human form was appropriate because it was the final work of creation (or the highest point of evolution so far, depending on the language which we wish to use).

Yet this account of God's response to death and suffering will only rarely satisfy a person who is in agony and whose intense suffering seems as if it will never end. Irrespective of whether their pain is physical, mental or psychological in its origin, for them, the simple explanation that the creation is 'fallen' and that they must share the consequences will not do – indeed it is insulting and patronizing for us to use it in their presence and expect them to accept it. Taken in conjunction with talk of a God of Love, it implies that although God may well love us, He is both powerless to act in our defense and has also made a number of significant errors in His work of creation. The universe is indeed flawed and they are paying the price for the shoddy workmanship. Arguments about rewards in heaven seem to be pious platitudes to people who feel that life is profoundly unfair.

If God is indeed both the God of Love and also powerful, then the answer to the question of suffering must have something to do with the fact that this apparently flawed universe actually is the best possible way in which a universe can be created, albeit that the cynic will then ask why God bothered at all if nothing better was possible. The bold claim which follows is that the very act of creation is such that, for creation to work, it has to contain these apparent flaws. If creation were to be otherwise and these apparent problems were to be removed or never have existed, then it must be the case that the consequences would have been even worse. God knew that there would be problems involved with creation, just as we know that there will be problems involved in building a house or designing a new model of car or in bringing up children in a way which is responsible and loving, but these problems do not usually stop us in our task.

This is the point made by Paul Fiddes when he states that God's contingency in creation is also His contingency in suffering. In each case God decides once and for all, but this is actually just one single choice.[13] God demonstrates His acceptance of these problems by the incarnation. God's coming in human form is to accept every facet of the limitations in His creation. We have seen how Jesus' death and resurrection deals with Sin and atonement. It is also true that the death of Jesus can be seen as God's acceptance of the laws of creation, as well as His cosmic victory through the resurrection and its promise that the whole creation will also experience such resurrection.[14]

Given our present interests, it is instructive to consider how the various theories of the atonement are capable of dealing with the questions of death, suffering and natural disaster and the theological consequences which follow if we apply a given theory of the atonement to these issues. It is a salient observation that despite the acute pastoral relevance of this question, it is one to which there is no readily available response. As we have already noted, there is the distinct possibility that the theory of the atonement which provides the most satisfactory answer to the question of suffering and the flawed universe is also the closest approximation to the truth and that a theory which cannot address these issues must be regarded as less than satisfactory. However, we must also remind ourselves that no theory should be thought of as providing us with the complete picture and that any judgment which we might make is being made by human standards.

The subjective view of the atonement, with its emphasis on a human change of attitude inspired by the example of Jesus' crucifixion, suggests that suffering is something to be endured, following the example of Jesus Christ. Because Christ suffered, this should help us to endure our own suffering and because Christ died, so we should also be enabled to face our own death. Such views are not uncommon in popular piety and pastoral advice and whilst there is undoubtedly a great deal of truth in them, it can often seem as if they are the only explanations of suffering which are offered by ministers who would not dream of adopting a subjective view of the atonement as a solution to the problem of Sin. This is not to deny that the crucified Christ can serve as an inspiration, but if the atonement is not merely subjective in nature then there needs to be more than this subjective model in our approach to death and suffering.

The objective view, with its emphasis on the fact that Christ actually did something for us and is not merely an inspiration, implies that, in some way, God is actually present within the suffering and within the death and that we are not left to rely on our own strength alone. Rather than being an external point on which we can focus as a source of comfort, God is actually present at the very point where the pain occurs and hits home. God is present with us in the suffering, God is with us throughout the process of dying and God is then with us in our rising to new life. It is possible that these ideas have been neglected in a pastoral context due to a reluctance to claim that God can experience pain.

Within the range of ideas which can be described as 'objective', substitutionary atonement emphasizes that death is not final because Christ died in our place. Because we are all well aware of the fact that we shall all die, the consequence of this theory is that there must therefore be new life beyond death. Looking at the ideas which exist within this framework, expiation would seem to emphasize the presence of God with us and propitiation to imply that there is no need for us to fear death and that no punishment will await us. It is hard to see how such a powerful and triple emphasis that God is with us in the pain, that there is no need to be afraid, and that a new life awaits us beyond death could be produced from the subjective view. No doubt proponents of the subjective view would be happy that such ideas cannot be suggested by their favored theory, for they would believe that at least part of this claim is erroneous. The use of such ideas within the pastoral care provided by a proponent of the subjective view would be theologically inconsistent but they should certainly form part of the theological toolbox used by a proponent of substitutionary atonement. Whether we hold a subjective view of the atonement or an objective view, there needs to be a consistency between our theology and our pastoral care.

The position on suffering which is produced by forensic justification or imputed atonement is less clear. When these theories are used in a pastoral approach to death and suffering, the emphasis appears to be more on hearing God's words of reassurance than on a faith that He has done something on our behalf. Perhaps the key is that neither theory should be regarded as self-sufficient. We do need to hear the news of what God has done through His own declaration to us, but a sufferer wants and needs to see action rather than merely hearing words – a fact which Job was quick to observe in his dialogue with his friends.

In terms of its pastoral implications, the 'classical view' seems to be the epitome of objective atonement. This is the case because it is here more than with any other theory that we find the assurance that God is truly with us in our pain and participates in the trauma of the creation. God is not merely an inspiration but is actually present with us and in us. Our suffering and the suffering of Christ are intermingled and He feels what we feel. Our death is a participation in His death, and our resurrection is thereby assured through a sharing in His resurrection, just as Paul explained to the readers of his letter to the Romans. The suffering and vulnerability of God have been discussed in a number of places, but we must be clear that this suffering and vulnerability is not a projection of human emotion or sentiment, nor must we create a helpless God who suffers as we do.[15] This must be a God who is victorious over human evil through making the choice of weakness. This is the God who experiences in Himself the apparent flaw in His creation. There can be no satisfactory theodicy which does not include an end to both physical and moral evil. Ultimately, the crucified Christ had to rise from the dead.

The present contention is that if love is demonstrated by 'being there', by sharing, by participating and by the laying down of one's life for one's friends, then it is the 'classical view' of the atonement which provides the most satisfactory response to the questions posed by death and suffering; the questions which any faith or philosophy of life has to be able to answer if it is to be relevant in the present day.

4.3 Entropy and Atonement

Salvation is about totality: it concerns everything. As Pannenberg notes, it is important that our picture of salvation incorporates this global view and includes the eschatological future of God, for this is the necessary corrective to the human tendency to focus on moral achievement by humanity in this world alone.[16] It is almost a truism that we can be saved only if we have first become lost, and Christians who deny that they are or were once lost have somehow missed the whole point. Whether or not we believe in the concept of Original Sin, we are bound to accept the Second Law of Thermodynamics, albeit that this does not preclude a naive and ill-fated optimism on the part of certain groups in society who seem to believe that human endeavor can still produce a perfect world. Salvation through God stands in bold opposition to such endeavor and to its ultimate failure in the face of the Second Law. As to why the world was created complete with the Second Law, this is a theological problem and is addressed in section 5.3 as well as in the final page of the book. Of course, this salvation which is to be found in Christ does not free us from earthly death – the Second Law is not annulled – but the Christian claim is that what is essentially us, ourselves, will be resurrected in a new body, beyond the existence which we experience at the present time, through our participation in the death and resurrection of Jesus Christ.

We have considered the way in which the various theories of the atonement can address the issues raised by death and suffering, as well as whether they are adequate to explain the forgiveness of our sins. We must now consider whether they are compatible with the Second Law of Thermodynamics and the insights which can be gained by considering the various theories in the light of this scientific statement.

The subjective view of the atonement, which we described as 'no-hope' theology in section 4.1 must still bear that label. It does so because, if we examine the picture of Jesus dying as an example to us rather than being involved in some form of decisive action for us and on our behalf, then all we are left with is the inspiration to battle against the effects of the Second Law. This is the claim that Jesus was subject to the law but that we can still try our best and hope to survive. This hope can be readily dismissed as no-one has ever succeeded in preventing the eventual and final death of any other human being. However good it is to fight against disease, injury and accidents within the finite nature of the human time scale, it is a clear fact that we shall all die in the end. The insight of the Second Law supports the contention that the subjective view of the atonement will not work.

If we now turn our attention to the objective view of the atonement, this implies that an outside agent removes the consequences of Sin and the Second Law at some point in our collective or personal history. It is here that the interplay of ideas between science and Christian doctrine is more productive and creative.

Substitutionary atonement presents us with the image of the crucified Christ suffering the effects of the Second Law, effects which by right belonged to us. The result is that for us they are no longer ultimately final in their effect. Whether there is any difference here between expiation and propitiation other than as is traditionally explained in theological arguments is unclear. Expiation can be expressed as the statement that Jesus becomes subject to the Second Law and suffers its effects so that having done its work it has no lasting effect on us. Propitiation is when God concludes that the long-term effects of the Second Law no longer apply to us because Jesus has suffered their ultimate consequence – a consequence which had to be borne by someone if God's own integrity was not to be violated. This latter approach now begins to sound contrived rather than distasteful. Both of these two variations suffer from the problem that although we have been saved from death we still have to die. Our life in this world is still finite. The Second Law still works its effects on us and we do pay some sort of price, even though we are repeatedly told that we have been saved. In terms of death, a cynic might describe substitutionary atonement as a grotesquely fictitious salvation.

Moving on to consider imputed atonement, we are presented with a pronouncement from God that we will not suffer the long-term consequences of the Second Law, albeit that these consequences will still affect us in this present life. Christ has shown that He can move beyond the Second Law, and God declares that those who are baptized in His name will also reach this place. This is totally in accord with the consequences of the Second Law of Thermodynamics and with the observation that although we might well have received the long-term status of 'saved', we still have to die. Indeed, it could be argued that this imputed (or fictitious) atonement makes far more sense when considered in this new light than it did when it was simply a response to sins and moral misdemeanors. Our understanding of the Second Law has again shed new light on traditional Christian doctrine.

The classical view, in which we participate in Christ's death and will therefore participate in His resurrection, finds expression in the statement that Christ became subject to the Second Law like us, in order that we can participate in His defeat of the Second Law through bodily resurrection. Of all the views or theories of the atonement, this is the easiest to apply to the idea that salvation is salvation from ultimate death rather than from having to suffer the consequences of moral misdeeds. It is therefore no surprise that it also fits neatly with the Second Law, since this is a statement about disorder and human mortality rather than about moral transgressions.

The conclusion is therefore that the subjective view of the atonement is incompatible with the parallels which appear to exist between Original Sin and the Second Law of Thermodynamics. The objective view is much more in keeping with these parallels, with the classical view seemingly providing the best fit of all. This is no surprise, for the classical view also emerged as the favored option in sections 4.1 & 4.2 and the author has a bias in this direction. However, to admit this bias is to be critically real and not to conceal an inbuilt prejudice. In this context the conclusion may be of more interest to the scientist than to the theologian.

4.4 Freedom and the Cross

We have already seen that when things go wrong, then it is possible to distinguish between what we have termed the effects of moral evil and physical evil in providing an explanation for the unsatisfactory course of events. In a theological discussion about death and suffering and the way in which these can be reconciled with belief in the God of Love, it is again helpful to draw this distinction between evils and disasters which result from human actions and those which occur due to natural disasters or incidents.

Death and suffering which are caused by human actions, whether these are deliberate as in an act of murder or accidental as in many everyday incidents, can be understood as having a cause which is based upon a faulty human decision. They can be described in theological terms as being a consequence of Original Sin or fallen human nature. For God to have prevented the incident would have involved His contravening the freedom which has been granted to the human race. It is a straightforward task to observe that the loss of this freedom would almost certainly be too heavy a price to pay for the removal of Original Sin from the universe.

Natural disasters, such as earthquakes, or certain illnesses which are due entirely to chance or to genetic predisposition, are less easy to explain in this scheme of things. Here, there is no erroneous choice made by a human being and no human freedom for God to violate if He is to act in order to prevent pain and suffering. Although we may well draw the conclusion that such events are evidence that the universe as a whole appears to share in our fallen human nature, this claim provides little comfort to those who are in distress, nor does it appear to preclude action on our behalf by the creator.[17] This scheme of things appears to contain the real flaw and if we accept that the universe has to be this way to allow for our freedom of action, it would appear to be a flaw in the purpose of God who fails to intervene.

However, there are two problems involved with our invoking divine intervention to prevent such natural disasters. The first objection is that it presupposes that the human race has a priority over the rest of the universe. This priority would imply that although human freedom should not be violated, in that God will not prevent human sins, this same principle should be denied to the rest of the creation, thereby forbidding such events as earthquakes. Such an objection may or may not be sustainable and depends upon the extent to which anthropocentrism is acceptable within our theological framework and how we interpret the divine injunction to the human race in the first chapter of Genesis.[18] It is also closely tied in with our understanding of ecology and our theology of caring for the creation.

However, the second objection to such divine action is stronger, in that such divine intervention might well result in a self-contradiction in the nature and actions of God. If the world is made or created by God and it works in a certain way, then divine intervention could result in the equivalent of God changing His mind or annulling the results of a prior action. This is not to state that God wills events such as an earthquake, cancer or cystic fibrosis, nor is it to preclude miracles by claiming that they can never occur, for we do not know which specific actions would constitute such a self-contradiction. It is rather to state that God cannot contradict His own rules for the running of the universe. Indeed, if we have faith that this is the best possible universe of its kind, then such action would inevitably result in more serious consequences in a different time and place.

This, then, is the outcome of a discussion into the distinction between suffering which is attributable to human decisions and that which occurs due to natural processes. The two common themes which connect these areas are both relevant to our discussion; firstly the Fall, and secondly, freedom. We have already seen how a fallen nature can be attributed to the whole universe and not only to humanity. A similar situation can apply to freedom, with suffering caused by human decisions resulting from the human freedom to make such decisions and suffering caused by natural processes resulting from the freedom which is inherent in the universe. This latter freedom is a manifestation of the fact that the disorder which is present within the universe increases with time. A traditional theological approach points to the Fall in both cases, with a fallen human nature or a fallen creation producing suffering. A more mechanistic approach to these two cases places the blame on the shoulders of freedom, irrespective of whether we believe in God and have to explain His apparent inaction.

In each case, this inherent freedom which provides the potential for pain and suffering also brings with it both the potential for creativity and newness. Human beings produce new inventions, literature, music and art. Nature evolves new forms of life and the cosmos changes as new stars are produced, supernova explode and old stars die. This is the freedom which is associated with a general increase in the entropy of the universe. In a theodicy which relies upon freedom of action to explain suffering, we find a direct parallel between the Fall, together with its implications for the universality of Sin, and the freedom which is implicit in the Second Law of Thermodynamics.

A modern way of stating the classical view of the atonement might be to claim that both Sin and natural disasters, together with their consequential pain, suffering and death, are made possible by the freedom which God has given to His creation. God is loving and generous, but the enjoyment of His gift also has side-effects. However, on the cross, in the person of God the

Son, He accepts the consequences of this freedom; He accepts the side-effects in Himself. Through our participation in this death we will also share in His victory over death and in the resurrection.

In more scientific terms, we could say that the increase in entropy or disorder which is a fundamental characteristic of the universe is the cause of suffering and of death. The question then, is whether the cross can also be seen as God accepting the consequences of the Second Law of Thermodynamics. Does the cross say something about human powerlessness in the face of entropy or disorder? Can the cross address the scientific description of the world as well as the theological view with its teaching on Sin? If the answer is 'yes' then this says something important about God and about the ways in which theology and the philosophy of science can inform each other in this area. Again, it is important to realize that this approach is not intended to provide a synthesis of the two fields of study nor to be simply a series of abstract theological ideas. It is as much about faith as about doctrine and about the way in which faith has to interact with what is seen, felt and understood if it is to be true to its roots.

5

Doctrine and the Second Law

The parallels which appear to exist between the Second Law of Thermodynamics and the doctrine of Original Sin clearly have implications for our understanding of atonement, death and suffering. It is within these specific areas of theology that these two important general principles from science and Christian doctrine find their most obvious applications as they address the fundamental questions of human existence. However, the particular relevance of their parallels in this particular context should not be allowed to distract us from the possibility that these parallels may have other implications for Christian doctrine beyond the more obvious areas which we have considered in earlier chapters. It might be the case that they are able to shed new light on other aspects of the Christian tradition. Any new understanding which we gain should not alter the content of our doctrines, but it may well affect the ways in which we understand the Christian faith and the ways in which we talk about it. This applies both to our discussions within the Christian faith and to our conversations with the wider world. We may find that such an understanding can help us to gain new insights into our faith and doctrine and that as a result, it may help us to explain what we believe.

In this chapter we shall begin to explore some of these implications and the consequences of our discussion so far. We shall begin with the doctrine of God, considering first the doctrine of the Holy Trinity, before moving this discussion to focus on some pertinent issues in Christology. The second doctrine we shall consider will be that of the resurrection: both the resurrection of Jesus Christ and the resurrection in more general terms. The final subject for our study will be that of creation. As we shall see, the celebration and understanding of the Eucharist also becomes relevant at this point. Throughout these discussions, the emphasis will very much be on the word 'begin'. There is a great deal of material here which can stimulate further exploration, and the present remarks are intended as no more than a few notes and observations which can form a starting point in that process. However, before we engage with these issues, we need to be clear that we have now entered a new stage in the overall discussion. We are now making a religious assumption, namely that the Being of God and the resurrection of Jesus Christ are part of our worldview. Our earlier questions as to whether the Second Law of Thermodynamics and Original Sin (as defined within the present study) have close parallels, or might even really be the same thing, can be asked irrespective of whether or not we assume a belief in God. This is the case because asking the question involves a study of the content of theology rather than developing theology itself. The discussion in the present chapter requires that we make this divine assumption, just as we have already been working with the assumption that the laws of science are constant and universal. It is important that we remember that scientific methodology requires its own step of faith, however obvious this universal constancy might seem at first sight.

There is also a second sense in which we have reached a new stage in our discussion, for until now we have been exploring the idea that the Second Law and Original Sin might be saying the same or a similar thing. Now we are beginning to consider the consequences which follow if this possible correlation is indeed the case. Can the Second Law of Thermodynamics also inform our discussion of other traditional Christian doctrines?

5.1 The Doctrine of God

The Christian doctrine of God is (or should be) about the Trinity, and so the first question which we need to address is whether the parallels between the Second Law of Thermodynamics and (Original) Sin are capable of shedding any new light on the doctrine of the Holy Trinity. How are we to relate the parallel between these two theories – one scientific and one theological – to God as Godself and what might we need to say about God if we take the Second Law seriously?

The first point which it is important to note is that we should recall that not only is the Christian doctrine of God the doctrine of God the Holy Trinity but that this Trinitarian declaration about God also implies that God is dynamic.[1] The second point to note is that, if we are writing from a Christian perspective, then our religious standpoint implies that we need to understand God as Being Itself or the ground of all being and not as a part of creation. This second point can sometimes be a matter of some debate within theological circles, but in the present context it does make a considerable difference. If God is a part of creation (or creation is a part of God) then God (or a part of God) must of necessity be subject to the Second Law of Thermodynamics. As we shall see in section 5.3, this would make the issue of salvation somewhat problematical. However, if God is external to creation then this problem does not arise. The fact that God consented to become part of creation in the incarnation makes the whole matter rather more profound and significant for the human race, but it does not destroy the fundamental principle that there is no problem in reconciling the Christian doctrine of God with the Second Law if God stands, at least in part, outside the created system.

The Trinity involves a self-distinction within God and, as Pannenberg notes, it is this self-distinction which makes the incarnation possible.[2] Indeed, it is only this self-distinction in the incarnation, where the God who is outside the Second Law accepts the limitations which this state of affairs brings with it, which makes salvation possible at all. It is only the triune nature of God which allows God to manifest His passionate concern for creation and for its fate under the conditions of the Second Law of Thermodynamics – only the Trinity allows God to be beyond creation and also within creation as a part of (human) history. There is nothing essentially new in what we are saying here. However, to say it explicitly about the Second Law of Thermodynamics rather than to repeat the claim that, in Jesus, God was subject to the constraints of human life, allows us to say it to new effect. We are not denying this claim, but are spelling out some of its consequences.

There is, however, an important point which it is worth noting and it is a point about subservience. It is a commonplace of Trinitarian doctrine that it runs the risk of lapsing either into modalism or into subordinationism.[3] In modalism we find a reduction of the three persons to three different modes in which God can exist. In subordinationism the Father is understood as being superior to both the Son and the Holy Spirit, whilst the Son is also often understood as being in some way superior to the Spirit. The error of adopting the ideas of subordination is perhaps understandable, given the nature of Jesus' discourses with His Father in John's Gospel. However, the key to avoiding this misunderstanding is to recall that in the Gospel this discussion centers on Jesus, not on the second person of the Trinity itself. Here in the incarnation it is the Son Himself who makes Himself subservient to the Father. This happens by the very nature of the incarnation and through Jesus therefore being subject to the Second Law. It also occurs because, having become incarnate, this is the only way for human beings to differentiate the person of Jesus from that of the Father. We must be clear that the vision of the Trinity which we are using in this book is one which excludes both subordinationism and modalism. If this approach could be described as being somewhat apophatic, in that we are describing God by what He is not, then this is nothing new within Christian theological tradition. Knowledge of God by denying that human concepts can be used to describe Him is an important aspect of the so-called *via negativa* which precedes the Christian faith and was brought to Christian prominence in the work of Dionysius.

If this approach appears to be verging into Christology, then so it should, and we do have some important explicitly Christological points to consider below, but if God is Trinity and Christology is the study of the second person of the Trinity, then the Trinity and God in God's own relationship is the true starting point for Christology. Traditionally, studies of Christology have been done either 'from above' or 'from below'. In the former case Jesus is assumed to be divine and only then is His humanity considered, and in the latter case the discussion begins with His humanity. However, if we place the discussion in a Trinitarian context then Christology should be done neither from above nor from below but from the starting point of the Trinity.[4] If we ask the question of the incarnate Word of God, then we cannot honestly ask it in isolation from God as God happens, and so we cannot ask it in isolation from the Trinity. If we cannot under- stand, for example, how the Son can be the Son without also considering the Father, or how Jesus could be anointed without also considering the Holy Spirit, then any Christology which restricts itself solely to Jesus Christ or the Word of God must, of necessity, be incomplete. If Christology is sometimes seen as confusing or as inadequate to answer the questions which are asked of it, then this is likely to be the reason why. Any Christological model which we construct needs to be robust enough to be mutually compatible and consistent with the doctrine of the Trinity. Deep in the heart of the one lies the other. God's being is God's becoming and God is only known as He becomes in relationship and within relationship. The true locus for Christological questing is that of the human encounter with the God-event, the becoming of God as Trinity: the human and the divine together, but always the divine as we find it in its own threefold indwelling and not as we might want it to be. This is our true divine presupposition for doing Christology.

Ultimately, of course, direct talk about the nature of God is a mystery. The mystery of God is what remains when the analogies which we use in our daily speech break down. It is, however, worth speculating just a little on the application of the Second Law of Thermodynamics to the Trinity itself. Strictly, this is an issue which we could ignore, for if we believe that God is, at least in part, beyond the universe (or creation) then He is not (wholly) subject to the Second Law of Thermodynamics and we have no need to indulge in such speculation. However, it is very tempting to metaphorically envisage the three mutually interpenetrating and interacting persons of the Trinity as existing in some kind of dynamic equilibrium. If we believe that the death of Jesus causes God pain, then this produces, in some way, a shift in that equilibrium – perhaps because God now embodies more disorder than before. This is certainly consistent with the theological notion that the tetragrammaton YHWH bears the implication that God is becoming what He will become. Indeed, perhaps it is in this becoming that God's salvation and re-creation in the world can be accommodated. Nowhere is God's becoming more explicit than in the person of Jesus.

The incarnation is, of course, about revelation and salvation – the salvation which we have already discussed in Chapter 4 when we considered the atonement. The incarnation is God's demonstration of His love for creation and His accepting of the consequences of the Second Law of Thermodynamics. It is here that the personal identity of Jesus takes shape, albeit that in the Easter event it is defined for all time. The Easter event is proleptic of the Kingdom of God and of salvation; it is about freedom from the Second Law (or Original Sin) as the love of God goes out and seeks that which is lost. There are a number of questions which arise at this point which we should address. Indeed, the first question for us to consider poses quite a problem, which is another way of saying that here there is the opportunity to discuss something of some considerable importance.

The incarnation is about the second person of the Trinity becoming human and coming to save that which was lost. To quote Athanasius, 'That which has not been assumed has not been saved.'[5] In other words, unless God takes human form, then God cannot save humanity; unless God takes material form, then He cannot redeem the creation. As a result, it has been our premise that Jesus, in His incarnation, is subject to the Second Law of Thermodynamics and is therefore able to die. However, if the Second Law of Thermodynamics is in some way an equivalent to Original Sin, then we have to answer the objection which asks how this can be, since we are clearly told that He was 'tested as we are, yet without sin'. In his New Testament writings, St Paul clearly understood Jesus as being a second Adam who had the purpose of freeing us from Sin. This raises the question as to how Jesus can be sinless and yet also be subject to the Second Law of Thermodynamics if the latter has some sort of correspondence to Original Sin. If Jesus failed to commit moral misdemeanors, then is it also true to claim that there was no overall increase in disorder associated with His life?

This is, of course, a new way of asking the question of how Jesus could be both truly God and truly man, and as such the process of answering the question might throw new light on this whole Christological issue. The question is right at the heart of the issue of Christology. We will begin by first clarifying this issue of Jesus' sinlessness.

Wolfhart Pannenberg has asked the important question as to where this idea of the sinlessness of Jesus really comes from. He argues that Jesus is the savior because of His death and resurrection, not because of any alleged sinlessness. 'Only as the crucified and risen Lord is he now and eschatologically definitive man.'[6] St Paul might have agreed, but would probably have gone on to note that the process only worked because of Jesus' sinlessness. As we have seen in Chapter 4, it is argued that the person who died in our place or for us had to be perfect.

The key to the solution to this puzzle lies in the distinction between Sin itself (what we have termed 'Original Sin') and sins as moral misdemeanors – a distinction which has long caused the church a great deal of confusion. A notable example of the confusion and the variation in language occurs in the Agnus Dei, verses derived from a statement of John the Baptist in St John's Gospel. In the Agnus Dei, the traditional English wording states, 'O Lamb of God, that takest away the sins of the world, have mercy on us', yet when we come to examine its origins in chapter 1 of St John's Gospel, John the Baptist sees Jesus and states, 'Here is the Lamb of God who takes away the sin of the world!' The biblical use of a singular noun which could be said to have an ontology of its own (Sin) has often been replaced in the liturgy by a plural noun (sins) which is then quite understandably read as referring to moral misdeeds. However, it cannot be the case that Jesus takes away all the moral misdemeanors in the world, partly because they still occur and partly because for Jesus to be truly human rules out the possibility of His being unable to commit such misdeeds (sins).[7] The Agnus Dei must surely be read in terms of Sin itself. Indeed, when the Church of England revised its liturgy and produced *Common Worship*, it made just such a change to the contemporary language version of the service of Holy Communion. Here the original singular noun of the Bible has been restored. The Lamb of God once again takes away the Sin of the world rather than its moral misdemeanors.

In contrast to the words of John the Baptist and the Agnus Dei, the statement that Jesus was 'tested as we are, yet without sin' is surely about moral misdeeds, because the temptation can only be real if there is the possibility of a consequent action. A better rendition of the English meaning might be 'tested as we are, yet without sinning'. Both here and in the statement of John the Baptist, we are saying that Jesus could have committed moral misdeeds but did not. This is the old contrast between *posse non peccare* and *non posse peccare* (being able not to sin and being unable to sin) which we saw in section 3.3. It is a statement that Jesus did not commit moral misdemeanors, but that He could have done so and that He was therefore subject to the Second Law of Thermodynamics. If we accept this particular understanding, then the apparent problem of the conflict between Original Sin and the Second Law which could have arisen in the life and person of Jesus Christ is resolved. Any argument that Jesus *could not* have sinned is surely docetism and denies His true humanity, but any argument that Jesus *did* sin denies His divinity. The humanity bestows the ability to sin and to experience temptation whilst the divinity bestows the ability to resist the temptation through the ability to not sin. The parallel argument in terms of the Second Law is that in His humanity Jesus had to expend energy and cause a net increase in disorder, but that in His divinity this increase could, in some way, be balanced out.

This account could appear to be heretical, partly because of the statement about Jesus and Sin and partly through the discussion of the divine and human natures. The answer to the question about Sin is that, as we noted above, within our present distinction between Original Sin and sins there is nothing immoral which is implicit in the idea of Original Sin. Original Sin is not a statement about moral or immoral actions or inactions. Original Sin is the universal state which allows humans (inevitably) to commit moral misdeeds or sins – it is the basic human condition in which we all share. It is a part of what both we and Teilhard de Chardin perceive as the flaw in creation. The point about Jesus is that, despite being subject to Original Sin and the Second Law, He did not commit moral misdeeds and it was this which led to His being fit to be our savior. If Jesus had been unable to commit moral misdeeds then He would not have been truly man, a belief which constitutes the heresy of docetism or Apollinarianism. Such a person cannot be a savior, for He would not have been human as we are and would not have shared our human condition. On the other hand, if – as a human being – He had been unable to resist temptations, then He would not have been truly divine, which is the heresy of adoptionism. The answer to the question of the two natures, the question of how Jesus can be both divine and human is that, if we accept the decision of the Councils of Ephesus and Chalcedon, then we have to achieve the appropriate balance within the person of Christ. At the one extreme we have to avoid the situation in which Jesus not only has two natures (human and divine) but is actually two persons joined together by a union of will (Nestorianism). At the other extreme we are to avoid the situation where the two natures disappear and there is only one remaining – that of the Divinity (the monophysite heresy). It could be thought to be rather remarkable that if we consider the various models for Christ put forward during the Christological controversy of the fourth and fifth centuries, then only the 'orthodox' outcome appears to be compatible with a universe which operates according to the Second Law of Thermodynamics. Another way of summarizing the whole of this argument might be to say that, in Christ, God accepts Sin without sinning and becomes subject to the Second Law of Thermodynamics in the knowledge that beyond its inevitable consequence of death lies the new life of the resurrection.

If we now broaden our Christological perspective so that we consider not only the person of Christ but also His work, then the miracles of Jesus provide us with an intriguing observation. These miracles are generally associated with healing and the overcoming of physical evil. In a few cases they are more explicitly a physical wonder of some sort. However, in both cases, they constitute a local decrease in disorder or entropy. In the individuals concerned, it is usually Sin which is seen to be overcome or conquered. However, we have connected Sin with the Second Law and the statement may be taken as equivalent. The miracles are effectively the creation of local pockets of order, presumably at the expense of disorder elsewhere. If the miracles are sometimes seen as God violating the laws of His own creation, then we must be clear that this is not the case. God does not violate the inbuilt laws of the universe. It is rather that the divine intervention seems able to make a highly unlikely event more probable at one particular place and time. The integrity of God and the consistency of science would both imply that there has to be a commensurate increase in disorder elsewhere – presumably in a non-living system.

5.2 The Doctrine of the Resurrection

The Christian faith teaches that Jesus Christ rose from the dead on the first Easter Sunday, two days after He had been crucified on the first Good Friday. As we discussed in the previous chapter, this has long been understood as God's response to the problems caused by human sinfulness and to the presence of Original Sin within the universe. However, given the discussion in the earlier chapters, we also need to ask what this teaching on the resurrection says about the Second Law of Thermodynamics. If there are definite parallels between the Second Law and Original Sin, then the resurrection must fit into the overall equation and must fit into it in such a way that it is consistent with the current understanding of both science and theology. How can the resurrection be possible if we accept, as we must, that the Second Law applies at all times and in all places? We cannot simply state that the Second Law is easily overcome under these special circumstances, for the Second Law of Thermodynamics summarizes the observation, which is taken to be a universal truth, that disorder in the universe increases with time. If this is the case then we cannot simply say that Jesus rose from the dead and thereby circumvented what has been seen and understood as a universal phenomenon. We have discovered significant parallels between the Second Law of Thermodynamics and Original Sin, but if these parallels are to be of any significance then we must also explain the apparent problems which can emerge as a result.

We begin our response with the observation that the resurrection of Jesus Christ appears at first sight to be an example of God's new creation, a subject which has been discussed in section 3.3 and which will appear again in section 5.3. One consequence of this claim is that the resurrection is possible because it is in one sense an ahistorical event which occurs outside time. However, the Christian church actually claims that the resurrection of Jesus Christ is an event which occurred within time and that it is a part of human history. If we want to state this more bluntly, we can say that the resurrection of Jesus Christ is an historical event and that we cannot bend the rules to suit our theological needs. In contrast, God's new creation is an activity which is often seen as occurring beyond time and which would therefore not be a part of human history in the way in which we would usually describe such history. The resurrection of Jesus Christ and God's new creation would therefore seem to be about different things.

Now it is possible for a theologian to argue that although the resurrection of Jesus Christ appears to be an event within human history, this is not actually the case. He or she could argue that the resurrection of Jesus Christ should be described as an example of prolepsis – an example of the future, however we may want to describe it, breaking into the present. In this case the prolepsis of the resurrection would be a foretaste of God's new creation entering into the present age. If we are to use the language of Karl Barth, it would be an example of *Geschichte* rather than of *Historie*.[8]

Unfortunately, the above argument appears to be a clear case of what we should be trying to avoid, namely a case of special pleading, with the theologian rewriting the rules to suit his or her own needs. The fact that, within the literary genre of science fiction, any description of a continuum from beyond time breaking into history and having unexpected consequences in the present would be seen as nothing out of the ordinary does nothing to invalidate this criticism. The theologian needs to be more rigorous than this, and he or she cannot plead the example of science fiction. It is also the case that we should be attempting to discuss reality rather than to engage in willful speculation.

Whether the above criticism and speculation is true or not, there is another possibility open to us. The Second Law of Thermodynamics states that disorder increases within a closed system and by no stretch of the imagination can a body left within a cave be considered as an example of a closed system as it is quite obviously open to interference by outside forces or objects. If we accept the existence of God (whatever that might mean), then within the terms of the Second Law of Thermodynamics it is surely in order for God to act as an outside agent and to apply the necessary energy for there to be a reordering which leads to a resurrection. All that is then necessary to balance this reordering is for the overall increase in disorder to end up somewhere else within the universe. Of course this means that God has, in this instance, violated human freedom by refusing to allow Jesus' death to be final. However, in theological terms this is simply to restate the common assertion that in the resurrection both physical and moral evil have been overcome or defeated.

According to Jürgen Moltmann, the resurrection of Jesus Christ is the preparatory and preliminary action of God in Jesus for the good of people and of the world. He notes that the resurrection is God's answer to both evil and to death.[9] If we wanted to rewrite Moltmann's statement in different language, we could claim that the resurrection is God's answer both to Original Sin and also to the Second Law of Thermodynamics. Original Sin and the Second Law of Thermodynamics encompass both physical and moral evil as well as death. In Teilhardian terms, the resurrection of Jesus Christ is God's answer to the 'flaw in the universe'. However, for Moltmann, it is not in the end the resurrection which changes the crucified Jesus into a saving figure but it is actually the resurrection which makes Him worthy of crucifixion in the first place. If Jesus was simply crucified and then died, this would achieve nothing, other than perhaps providing a short-term scapegoat. It is only the claim that He did rise, and that through resurrection He demonstrated that neither death nor Sin need have the final say, that makes His crucifixion worthwhile. It is only the resurrection which gives any significance to Jesus' life, shows His true nature and makes it worth the while of the authorities to attempt to get rid of Him. The resurrection is the proof that this was not just another Roman execution of a criminal, but an event of a different quality and magnitude altogether.

In his book on the Gospel of St John, Barnabas Lindars makes the point that Jesus' death and resurrection are the cosmic event to usher in the eschatological age.[10] Lindars states that in the person of Jesus, the devil's grip on humanity is broken and the victory over the 'ruler of this world' is won. We could rephrase (or demythologize) this statement by the claim that Original Sin has been overcome. However, if we wanted to demythologize these statements completely, then we could take them to mean that the Second Law of Thermodynamics need have no eternal effect.

This discussion has led us to the point where there are two issues which we must address. The first is the frequently asked question as to whether the resurrection can be considered as an historical event in our usual understanding of the term and, if this is the case, whether there are any wider consequences which arise from the present discussion. The second is that the resurrection is usually seen as bearing consequences for the human race and indeed for the whole creation and that we might therefore need to say something about this in the light of our discussion. What does it mean to claim that the Second Law of Thermodynamics need have no eternal effect? We may well have demythologized Lindars, but we still need to unpack the science. We should also note that although the traditional Christian belief is in an historical resurrection and that this offers more scope for us to pursue the current theme, in some ways it would be less problematical if the resurrection was seen as ahistorical. An ahistorical resurrection is less of a problem to reconcile with our usual experience from daily life, which is that dead people stay dead.

According to William James, it is the practical which matters rather than the speculation of theologians.[11] We could put this another way, stating that all true theology has to be the result of a personal encounter with God. There can be no true theology which is secondhand theology. If this is the case, then it turns the tables on the question of the historicity of the resurrection, for we must then either take the resurrection on trust or else we must reject it, but either way we should not ask for any theoretical proof. However, if we do take the resurrection on trust, then rather than attempting to justify it, we have instead to attempt to reconcile two very different sets of observations, namely those of the resurrection and those of the Second Law of Thermodynamics.

Death and decay and the consequences of human evil both confront us within the world. According to the claims made by Christian theologians, the resurrection of Jesus Christ provides the answer to both of these problems. In theological terms it provides the answer to Original Sin, as well as the answer to the death and decay – the same death and decay which we have seen are caused by the Second Law. Of course, if these two concepts are really different expressions of the same truth, then it is hardly surprising that the resurrection answers both questions. If we can accept the resurrection as history and accept the Christian interpretation of its consequences, then it is also the scientific answer to moral evil as well as to the death and decay which we associate with physical evil. The question is whether we should take the resurrection on trust and treat it as an historical event. There may also be a second question as to whether this alleged historicity must be established using the usual methods of historical enquiry which emerged during the nineteenth century.

The rise of historical methodology was welcomed by many theologians of liberal tendencies because they felt that it would finally allow them to delve back to the facts about the historical Jesus. However, the results of this quest did not fulfill their hopes. In some cases, the conclusions which they drew were negative, and most of the accounts of the life of Jesus which were produced differed quite markedly from each other. What was to become known as the 'old quest' for the historical Jesus was effectively killed off by Albert Schweitzer and others who concluded not only that the quest was a failure, but also that Jesus was deluded, and differed very little from ourselves.[12] The historical studies of Jesus in the twentieth century were associated largely with backtracking, a defense of Christian belief, and a recourse to the argument that history will not do the job anyway, because it is really a matter of faith. Debate on the historicity of the resurrection also fits into this general scheme.

The Baptist theologian Paul Fiddes sees this divorce of faith and history as remarkable. He notes the call of Rudolf Bultmann for a response to *kerygma* in the present time and reminds us of Karl Barth's talk of the experience of the encounter with God's Word in the present day. According to Fiddes, the trend to divorce faith from historicity devalues two thousand years of Christian experience as well as the further background provided by the experience of Jewish religion and the Old Testament scriptures. It ignores the historical detail provided in Luke's Gospel, where an attempt is made to ground the accounts of Jesus' life in the facticity of both space and time. It also ignores the possibility that, by the standards of their own day, the resurrection accounts of Paul and the evangelists were as near to written verification as would ever have been expected, albeit that there may have been a very different conceptuality involved. Rather than being defensive and wondering whether we can claim the resurrection as an historical event, Fiddes believes that Christianity needs to be far more positive.[13] Tom Torrance would appear to agree, for instead of us trying to fit the resurrection into each worldview which we consider, he believes that we must work out the possible implications for a worldview which explicitly includes the resurrection as an accepted fact and then examine the consequences.[14] In other words, rather than asking whether our general worldview can accommodate the resurrection, we need to work with a Christian worldview which takes it as a given fact, as without the resurrection there would be no Christian faith and none of the present questions would arise. Christian theology should operate from the perspective of a Christian worldview. If we do then examine the world from a Christian perspective, we have to assume the resurrection, just as when we use a scientific perspective, we make certain assumptions about scientific laws. Hopefully it is possible to do both of these things together. In a sense, this is our present question. What is the significance of the resurrection as an accepted historical event within a worldview which also includes the explicit acceptance of the Second Law of Thermodynamics as an essential fact of life?

In asking what constitutes an historical event, it is still commonplace to apply the three principles of historicity which were first put forward by Ernst Troelsch, albeit that this application often goes unrecognized and is therefore also unchallenged. Since we are considering historical events, it is important that we note the content and consequences of these principles. The first of Troelsch's principles states that historical criticism can neither prove nor disprove an event but rather that it gives a measure of the possibility of that event. This is important because it implies that historical criticism cannot discount the resurrection as an historical event nor, of course, can the resurrection ever be proved. For this reason, within a Troelschian framework, any claims that the resurrection cannot be called an historical event, in any plausible sense of the word 'historical', run contrary to the whole concept of historicity.

Troelsch's second principle is based on the idea of analogy, that is, that we have to suppose that general experience in the past is similar to general experience in the present. This is an example of the wider scientific claim that the laws of the universe are the same at all places and at all times. Here the facticity of the resurrection is somewhat more dubious as we are not used to experiencing resurrection events at all and it might seem that we may therefore need to discount that of Jesus. However, people were not used to encountering resurrection events two thousand years ago either, and in any case, when we discuss the resurrection of Jesus we are considering both a one-off event (at least so far) and an event involving someone who we also claim is divine. This may sound like special pleading, but the second principle of historicity could well be interpreted not as denying the resurrection, but rather as implying that we have to examine claims of Jesus' divinity in the light of His resurrection or vice-versa. We do not have a general experience, whether past or present, as to what happens when someone who is clearly human and also believed to be divine is put to death.

Troelsch's third principle is the principle of correlation, the idea that historical events are not isolated incidents but that there is a cause and effect in operation and that each event in history affects all others. The Christian perspective on the resurrection would be exactly the same. The resurrection is not an isolated event devoid of significance or meaning. The resurrection had a meaning when it occurred and it must also have had consequences which applied at that time, as well as consequences which apply to us in the present day.

Now, of course, these historical principles put forward by Troelsch presuppose a particular worldview. This worldview may or may not be that in which Christian theology operates, and if the application of these principles did result in a refutation of the resurrection, then the Christian theologian might put forward an alternative framework which presupposes the resurrection and which could be thought to be equally valid. It is important to realize that we cannot prove the factual historicity of the resurrection, albeit that we are called to have a faith that the resurrection is factually historical. This claim, however, presupposes the question as to whether an event must be proved according to the principles of Troelsch in order to be called historical.

The classical answer of the historian to this question would be 'yes, it does', whereas the person of faith might say 'no, it does not'. However, there is a need to hold faith and history together. All history is based on interpretation, and all accounts are subject to the presuppositions and subjectivity of the person who records them. This much is obvious, for it is simply to restate the fact that we live in a world where critical realism is the dominant method of interpretation whether we realize that this is the case or not. Indeed, we might argue that if God was wholly open to historical investigation then this would make God wholly an object. The real truth is probably that historical enquiry, at least in its usual form, is not the appropriate tool to investigate the resurrection. Above all, Troelsch's principles seem to preclude the occurrence of events which are unique and the Christian claim is that the resurrection of Jesus Christ is indeed an event that is unique in the history of the world to date. These two little words 'to date' are so important, for our interest lies primarily in what happens next – our interest lies in the sequel to these events and the theology of the sequel.

The whole subject of historicity and of the historical

worldview is in many ways based upon classical realism and has not been modified in the light of the changes in scientific approach which have occurred both with the advent of an understanding of space-time and also with the implicit rise of critical realism as the dominant scientific tool. The resurrection becomes far more plausible if we see it as an event in space-time rather than an event in a classically real world. This may sound as though we are repeating the claims about science fiction made earlier but perhaps it is just that science fiction has, almost by definition, a tendency to be based upon scientific development. Although this is not the place to provide any sort of definitive answer or detailed discussion, the concept of space-time does lend serious credence to the notion of prolepsis, where a future event breaks in upon the present.

However, there is an alternative approach to the discussion of the resurrection and its place in history when we undertake this discussion within the present context. Up to this point, the discussion has focused on the treatment of the resurrection which is obtained by applying Troelsch's historical methodology together with a brief account of some of the responses which can be made to this approach. We have examined how we might be able to call the resurrection 'historical' within these criteria. However, if we accept the resurrection as an *a priori* historical event, whether this be through prolepsis or otherwise, then we are in the position to ask what is for us a far more potent question. What is then the relationship between the resurrection and the Second Law of Thermodynamics?

Under these circumstances the answers to our questions become much clearer. There is the clear implication that if we accept both the Second Law of Thermodynamics and the resurrection as facts – and as Christians who accept the results of scientific endeavor that must be our position – then we are compelled by the former to accept that some form of external influence was responsible for the latter. Yet this statement claims no more than a restatement of traditional Christian faith, namely the belief that God raised Jesus Christ from the dead. Not that this is by any means a proof of the resurrection; it is simply a demonstration that there are no inherent discrepancies within the framework which we have constructed. The real questions raise their heads once more when we come to examine the issues of re-creation and the general resurrection.

In Christian doctrine, the resurrection of Jesus Christ is put forward as an event of cosmic proportions and implications, as well as a foretaste of what is to come. However, although it is easy to reconcile the resurrection of one body with the Second Law, it becomes much more difficult when we consider the resurrection in more general terms and ask about the renewal of the whole universe. The re-creation or reordering of a closed system would appear to run contrary to the whole idea of the Second Law of Thermodynamics. It is time for us to consider the creation itself and with it the subject of the eschatological re-creation – the way in which God will make all things new at the end of time.

5.3 The Doctrine of Creation

The doctrine of the creation has been implicit in much of our discussion.[15] We have been working with the assumption that if God, in some way, created the universe, then the Second Law of Thermodynamics was and is part of that creation. In addition, we have also considered the way in which the atonement provides a response to what we perceive as the unfortunate side-effects of a universe which operates in this way – a universe which seems to contain a flaw which manifests itself as both physical and moral evil. This raises the issue as to why the Second Law of Thermodynamics was necessary in the first place. If the universe just happened to be this way then that might be considered to be unfortunate, but that is a rather different situation to one in which there is a divine purpose at work and in which we might feel justified in asking why such a law was necessary. Whilst we might be able to agree that the key to theodicy has to do with God's acceptance of the human condition at the incarnation and in His crucifixion, there still remains the much-asked question as to why God did not create a better world which did not have this flaw, so that pain, suffering and natural disasters did not occur in the first place.[16] There is also the question as to how God can ultimately renew the creation at the end of time. Does such a re-creation contravene the Second Law of Thermodynamics? We shall begin with this second question of re-creation and then return to the nature of the world as we experience it in the present day.

At first sight, the reconciliation of the Second Law and eschatological re-creation might appear to be a relatively straightforward issue. If the whole of the universe is to be renewed, as Christian theology often claims, then we have to resolve the issue of how the universe – which is scientifically understood as a closed system – is to receive the necessary input of energy to enable this reordering to occur.

The facile answer to the question is to state that although the universe is indeed a closed system from the present scientific perspective, God is not a part of the universe and that in this sense, when God acts, the universe is not closed. It must be noted that we should not state that God is outside the universe, for this is a statement which assumes that we are dealing with a conventional picture of space. The truth is that we do not know how to talk about something which is not a part of the universe any more than we know how to refer to God before time was created (or, more correctly, when time was not). It should also be noted that this is not an attempt to prove the existence of God nor is it an attempt to use God to fill a gap in our knowledge. God has already been invoked through our religious assumption and by our question about the renewal of creation within a closed system. It is our introduction of God into the discussion which has raised this question in the first place. If we remove the concept of God from our discussions then we no longer have an eschatological re-creation for which we need to account, just as if we remove the assumption that the universe is a closed system, then there is no problem with the concept of renewal – at least not from the point of view of the Second Law of Thermodynamics.

Now the above answer, namely that God is not a part of the universe, does indeed appear to be simple and straightforward. However, it also begs two further questions, both of them questions for the theologian who has to live in a universe where the Second Law of Thermodynamics describes the way things are and who needs his or her theological discussions to take account of the scientific description of the world. The first of these questions concerns the consequences of God not being part of the universe (or creation) and the second concerns the question of universal (or general) salvation. We shall consider the issue of salvation first, before turning to the issue of the relationship between God and the universe.

It is an age-old theme of Christian theology as to whether salvation is simply for the chosen few or whether it is for us all. This can be restated as the question as to whether the death of Jesus Christ on the cross and His subsequent resurrection brings the promise of new life to all people who have ever lived on earth, or whether it comes only to those who have been baptized or possibly to some smaller and specially select group within the circle of the baptized. If salvation is for all people, then the question can be extended to ask whether this is salvation for the whole of the creation (the whole universe) or whether it is only for the members of the human race here on earth.

The answer to this question on the subject of salvation is of great importance because of what it can tell us about our understanding of God. The God who will only grant salvation to a small group of people – perhaps to some subset of those who have been baptized – is clearly not only a very selective God, but also a God whose power might be thought to be somewhat limited. If renewal or re-creation is to apply only to a very small part of creation (and this would be a minuscule part indeed) then the implications of the Second Law of Thermodynamics pose no problem. If only a very small part of a closed system is to be reordered, then the necessary decrease in entropy can easily be found by an increase elsewhere within that system. The same consideration would also apply if re-creation were to apply to all people on earth, or indeed to the whole of the earth itself and all it contains. The earth is very small in comparison to the whole universe, and the constraints inherent within the Second Law of Thermodynamics would pose no problem to the God who wishes to carry out such a reordering. On the cosmic scale of things, it is far less significant than tidying the living room or redecorating a house.

On the other hand, if we are to envisage a God who renews the whole creation (i.e. the whole of the universe), then not only is this a far grander view of the power of God, but it also requires that there is a sense in which God must be separate from the universe. The whole of a closed system cannot be reordered, at least not the whole of any closed system which we can understand, for such ordering must, by definition, take place from within. Unlike a selective doctrine of salvation, when God can be part of the universe, universal salvation precludes this possibility and God has in some sense to be separate. In colloquial terms, we might say that any old god can save a few people or the members of a particular religious sect, but it takes the Real God to renew the whole universe.

Although his view of cosmology was somewhat different to that which we hold in the present day, St Paul clearly shared the latter vision where the salvation wrought in Jesus Christ was for everything. As he wrote in chapter 8 verses 19–23 of his letter to the church at Rome:

For the creation waits with eager longing for the revealing of the children of God; for the creation was subjected to futility, not of its own will but by the will of the one who subjected it, in hope that the creation itself will be set free from its bondage to decay and will obtain the freedom of the glory of the children of God. We know that the whole creation has been groaning in labor pains until now; and not only the creation, but we ourselves, who have the first fruits of the Spirit, groan inwardly while we wait for adoption, the redemption of our bodies.

This discussion is quite revealing, because in everyday thought it quite often seems to be the case that those Christians who hold a selective understanding of salvation (on the grounds of baptism or whatever else) also have a greater vision of the power of God, whereas those who hold a universal or more general under-standing of salvation also appear to have a lower doctrine of God's creativity and power. However, the conclusions which emerge from our discussion turn this state of affairs on its head. They quite clearly imply that not only is universal salvation consistent with greater power in itself (simply because it involves the re-creation of more people) but that it is also consistent with a greater understanding of the power of God from a viewpoint which includes the Second Law of Thermodynamics. Indeed, if we are to understand creation and salvation as different sides of the same coin, then this should come as no surprise. The renewal of the whole creation (and the salvation of all people) gives a much grander view of God than the salvation of a (very small) subsection of humanity who can satisfy what can often be a demanding and detailed list of quali-fications.

We now return to the question of the relationship between God's being and the being of the universe. We first note that the being of God (who is often understood within Christian theology as 'Being Itself') is a subject beyond the scope of the present work. However, although the tradition in Christian theology has been that the creation is separate to God (albeit that God took flesh in Jesus and indwells the creation through the Holy Spirit), there has also been a persistent minority view that the creation is in some way a part of God – the idea of panentheism. This idea was widely discussed in patristic times, and found re-expression in the twentieth century through process theology. It essentially means what it says, namely that everything is within God. It should be distinguished from the concept of pantheism which identifies everything with God.[17] When they are viewed from the perspective of the Second Law of Thermodynamics, both traditional doctrine and panentheism allow God to renew the creation. A creation which is separate from God can be renewed, as could a creation which is a part of God or within God. However, from the perspective of the Second Law, a creation which is identified with God would be excluded from this possibility.

This consequence should be quite clear from a consideration of our earlier discussion. A God who is identified with the universe or who dwells wholly within this universe cannot renew the whole universe because He is a part of this closed system. Yet such renewal is one of the oft-quoted claims of Christian theology. This has serious consequences for pantheism – the technical name for the identity of the universe with God. Within this scheme of things, pantheism can hold out no ultimate hope, for it cannot overcome the Second Law of Thermodynamics. It does not matter what we try to do within a closed system; disorder continues to increase. It would seem that a theologian who advocates pantheism cannot also claim universal salvation.

These same claims would also seem to apply to the so-called Gaia hypothesis which has grown from an idea of James Lovelock in the 1970s.[18] Lovelock made a major contribution to atmospheric chemistry through his development of electron capture mass spectrometry. This allowed the measurement of halocarbons in the stratosphere and provided the evidence and impetus for his subsequent prediction that these halocarbons would accumulate in the atmosphere and could damage the protective ozone layer in the stratosphere – a prediction which was later shown to be correct. At a later date he developed his Gaia hypothesis, an idea which is worth mentioning because it has gained some popularity in the dialogue between theology and science, albeit rather more from theologians who are interested in science than from scientists who have trained in theology. In the Gaia hypothesis, the ecosystem of the earth is seen as a single entity in its own right; an entity which tends to work for its own self-preservation. However, if it is to be treated as a closed system then it is doomed by the Second Law of Thermodynamics and if it is an open system (which it clearly is, due to the input of sunlight) then Gaia loses any notion of self-sufficiency. The parallels in which Gaia is likened to some form of deity, which many followers of the idea seem to presuppose, become rather devalued.

What is clear from the present considerations is that the Second Law of Thermodynamics leads us to a grander vision of God if our vision of God begins from the assumption that Jesus Christ rose from the dead and that God wills the renewal of His creation. If we consider the way in which the universe works, then it is clear that God has in some sense to be beyond the universe.

Looking at matters more widely, it could even be the case that a healthy respect for science can help to prevent theologians from following erroneous pathways as they seek to describe God. Science tells us about the universe and hence about the revealed doctrine of God. Such revelation is not associated with a direct impartation of knowledge, nor is it a reinvention of the argument for the existence of God from design in the way in which it is commonly understood.[19] If we make the religious or theological assumption of a creative God, then that God must be consistent with the way in which we understand the universe.

This returns us to the question with which we began this section; a question which theology has to attempt to reply. This is the question as to why God would create a world which is flawed; a world in which pain and suffering appear to be unavoidable. Without these apparent deficiencies the whole enterprise of the eschatological re-creation which we have been considering would be unnecessary. Why is there all this pain and suffering?

The usual answer given to this question is that this is the best of all possible worlds. The understandable retort to that correct but superficial answer is that in that case God might as well not have bothered. Indeed, Athanasius observed that without some form of solution, this was the logical conclusion to draw. 'Surely it would have been better never to have been created than to be neglected and perish,' he wrote.[20] The response noted above, namely that this is the best possible world, brings with it the assumption that free will is high on the list of priorities. We have the ability to make real decisions about our lives and our future and this ability also includes the possibility of committing deliberate acts of ill-will. The possibilities inherent in this view of human freedom and moral evil are partnered by those of physical evil and disaster in the natural world. The claim is then made that without this possibility of making real decisions about our lives and human conduct in the world, any possible lack of pain and disaster would not be worth having.

This is a perfectly valid viewpoint as far as it goes and it is a standard approach to the subject. However, it might well be a dialogue which is both unnecessary and which also reveals a lack of scientific understanding. If Stephen Hawking is correct, and intelligent life can only exist in a universe in which entropy increases (in other words, the Second Law of Thermodynamics as we have described it is essential for life to exist). then in order for

God to create thinking beings (with whatever nuance we wish to place on the word 'create') the Second Law has to describe the universe. It is only possible for us to exist in a universe which follows the principles which we call the Second Law of Thermodynamics. Without the state of nature which is described by that law, we would not be here. This is the clear scientific claim that physical evil is unavoidable and we know all too well that moral evil is also present. We might put this in another way by stating that without our Teilhardian flaw in the universe, there would be no-one around to notice the so-called perfection which would then be present. God's answer to the problem which this situation produces, namely freedom at the expense of the presence of evil, then comes in His Son, for His response cannot be built into any created system. The problem can only be solved by that which is not created and that must mean God Himself.

This approach may solve one problem, but it also appears to create another. Because both physical and moral evil are unavoidable, are we therefore obliged to say that they were created by God? An alternative way of putting this is to ask whether God created Original Sin. Whichever way we ask the question, we need to examine the consequences of such a creative act. However, we should note that an overall increase in disorder can, in fact, also give rise to a local increase in order, an effect demonstrated in the thermodynamics of certain chemical systems.[21]

The first point to make in response is that it is a mistake to equate deliberate acts of ill-will or moral evil with Original Sin. Original Sin (as we have described it) is a state of being in which it is possible for errors to be made and moral misdeeds to be committed. In terms of classical dualistic language, and echoing St Paul in his letter to the church at Rome, we could say that Original Sin is that state in which forces for good wish us to do good and forces for evil wish us to do evil. We are at liberty to follow either course and from time to time we follow the latter. Nevertheless the question as to whether God created Original Sin will not go away. We are certainly claiming that God produced the situation which we describe using the Second Law of Thermodynamics as a necessary part of creation. If Original Sin is equivalent to the Second Law of Thermodynamics, then it follows that God created this too: although it is important for us to remember that, in our terms, Original Sin is morally neutral. In short, the creative God creates and then has to solve the problems which He already knew would be present. The rest, as is sometimes said, is history, as God enters the world as the Son.

We should also remind ourselves that things can go wrong both as a result of human decision and also as a result of natural events. As we have seen in Chapter 1, this is what John Polkinghorne sees as the distinction between moral evil and physical evil and we have used these terms throughout our discussion.[22] Physical evil occurs as the consequence of a world exploring and realizing its own potentiality and is a consequence of the Second Law of Thermodynamics. Moral evil is the failure to accept creaturely status which came about at some point in the development of human consciousness. In terms of our present language, then, physical evil can be equated to Original Sin and the Second Law of Thermodynamics, whilst moral evil can be equated to moral misdemeanors or sins. Original Sin is not merely a concept which has been noticed by human beings and which describes their propensity to commit moral misdemeanors. It is applicable to the whole universe, describing the natural disasters which occur in a system which is driven by the impetus to maximize the disorder which is present.

It is in God's acceptance of the physicality of the universe in His own self that we find the ultimate reconciliation of physical evil and Original Sin with the idea that God is Love. Even so, the realization that the creation had to be this way, because entropy has to increase with time if intelligent life is to exist, is still a difficult idea to accept. We still wonder why there could not be a better universe without this apparent flaw. The same applies to the re-creation which we are promised, even if this does sound like the proverbial pie-in-the-sky. Perhaps it is in the questioning that we find the possibility of receiving an answer. The possibility comes when we ask the question 'Why, God, why?' rather than asking the question in some abstract way about God in the third person. When Job dared to question God, he obtained a response despite the criticism of his friends who counseled that God would not answer. Jesus Himself asked His Father, 'Why have you forsaken me?'

If there is an earthly answer to the question – and we should not be complacent and assume that there necessarily is – then perhaps it is in the concept of Eucharist that this final answer resides. This answer will be related to the promise, made real in the Eucharist, of just what it is that can be realized when God's plans and purposes have been achieved. We must therefore turn our attention to the Eucharist, although we shall have cause to revisit the subject as to why the Second Law was necessary when we reach the latter part of Chapter 6. This is the point at which we shall finally close our exploration by revisiting the Garden of Eden.

5.4 The Eucharist

We have already quoted the words of the Agnus Dei, but it is worth repeating them: 'O Lamb of God, that takest away the sin(s) of the world, have mercy upon us.' These words, which are usually said or sung as a part of the Eucharist or service of Holy Communion, speak to us of the role of Christ in the universe. They speak to us of the future life of which the bread and the wine which we receive at the Eucharist are but a foretaste. However, as we have noted above, it is somewhat unfortunate that in many versions of the liturgy, that which is taken away is described by the word 'sins', rather than the word 'Sin' – the word which we find when we examine the original wording in chapter 1 of John's Gospel. It is unfortunate, because it is this fallenness, this decay, this tendency for things to go wrong, the flaw in the universe, which is taken away, rather than the moral misdeeds or misdemeanors which occur as a consequence of the underlying condition. For 'the sin of the world' (but not 'sins'), perhaps read 'the Second Law of Thermodynamics'. There is a sense in which this removal of the state of Sin – the fallenness of the creation, the flaw, this physical evil as it is sometimes described – is a prolepsis of the end. This is the final Easter made present here and now – for Easter is our end; it is where we are going. The Christian church is an Easter people and 'Alleluia' is our song.

This idea has been well summed up by Olivier Clement.

The world was created as an act of celebration, so that it might share in grace and become Eucharist through the offerings of human beings. And that is precisely what Christ, the last Adam, has accomplished. By his death and resurrection he has brought glory to the universe. It is this transfigured creation that is offered to us in the Eucharist in order that we too may be able to join in this work of resurrection.[23]

The bread and the wine are transfigured, so that whatever else they may or may not be, they do in some sense belong not to this world, but to a different world – to the Kingdom of God in its fullness. They enter into this fallen world and express life without Sin or the Second Law of Thermodynamics. Each of us can choose to accept them and we can choose to accept them either in this spirit of the foretaste of a new world in which the love of God reigns supreme, or in a spirit in which we still bear enmity against our neighbor.

Written in this way, it all seems quite easy, but forgiveness is a costly business and forgiveness involves not only a forgiving of moral transgressions but also involves a moving on, so that the whole system which allowed the transgressions to occur is involved in the process. Sometimes, even in human terms, our wrong actions are the result of forces which are beyond our control. Nicholas Lash makes the point that: 'Forgiveness is not forgetting, but addressing as "You" another who has hitherto only known the forgiving one as an it.'[24]

In other words, forgiveness involves a change of relationships. In being forgiven we enter into a new relationship and we treat the person who forgives us with love and proper justice. Indeed, in tying together Easter and forgiveness, Lash makes the point that the rich always need the permission of the poor, and the victor always needs the forgiveness of the victim, if they are to be able to sing the Easter song of 'Alleluia'.

Nowhere is this truer than in the forgiveness of God and in the renewal of the world as His Kingdom. It is true in this case not only because God is God and because He addresses us as 'you' but also because to think of God in the third person is to evade the very issue of God. Lash quotes Martin Buber, who wrote that: 'God is the You that in accordance with its nature cannot become an it. If to believe in God means to be able to talk about him in the third person, then I do not believe in God.'[25]

Our relationship with God is not that of an 'it', for God calls us 'you'. If this is the way in which God speaks to us, then we are compelled to address Him. This is the God whose ultimate purpose is to take away the Sin of the world – that failing physicality which is tied up with the Second Law of Thermodynamics. He does this through a new creation which can only be expressed because neither God nor we are an 'it'. This is the situation in which we come to worship God and to share in His glory. In the new creation, that sharing will finally be complete as we participate in God. This is not to claim that we will become lost within God as is the case in the beliefs of some mystical and Eastern religions, but that we can share completely with God.

Our being made in the image of God is a statement of this fact, that we are called to grow into communion with Him. It has nothing to do with morality but is a statement of our potential for perfect communion with God, a communion which occurs when Original Sin is no more and the creation is renewed so that the Second Law of Thermodynamics is no more either.

In the Eucharist God grants us a foretaste of this new state when 'he will wipe away every tear from their eyes. Death will be no more; mourning and crying and pain will be no more, for the first things have passed away' (Revelation chapter 21 verse 4). At its best, the Eucharist is our being with God. We receive the bread and the wine not because of what we know or do or say; not because we have passed some sort of test; but simply because of who we are. We are people whom God addresses as 'you'; we are people who are made both in His image and in His likeness and who are on their way home.

6

Where Do We Go From Here?

6.1 Experience or Faith? Science and Theology Revisited

We have nearly reached the end of our discussion and we therefore need to make a few comments about the way forward. However, there is a final question which is pertinent to any dialogue between science and religion, as well as to the reader of a book which contains what may appear to be novel ideas. This is the question of whether we want to base our decisions upon personal experience or whether we want to take things on trust and to accept information by faith. It is important to note that science relies on the latter approach. Science is based on faith, because most people in the world are not engaged in scientific research and can therefore only know about its results at second hand, by report or through the use of everyday objects which apply scientific principles. It may seem surprising that science relies on faith, but most practicing scientists work in a very restricted field and therefore have to make daily judgments of faith in accepting the work and results of their colleagues. In contrast to this application of faith, religion can actually offer the former approach, in that we can try it and see for ourselves. We are invited to participate in worship and to enter into a relationship with the Living God. We are offered the opportunity for personal experiences; we are offered the bread and the wine. However, as we have already noted in Chapter 3, this invitation is accepted on relatively few occasions.

Nevertheless, it is important that we should remember that the sort of personal experience referred to above is not the same as so-called objective knowledge. Learning by personal experience or by the results of experimentation is about entering into a worldview and accepting the assumptions of that worldview, with all the resulting implications, ways of operating and of thinking which it entails. In any form of experimentation, we bring with us various assumptions which are necessary in order to run the experiment, and the results cannot be isolated. Whenever we truly enter into relationship, whether it be with God, with human beings or with the world through the medium of science, we ourselves are also open to being changed.

We began our journey by observing the apparent similarities between the concept of Original Sin and the Second Law of Thermodynamics and then continued by asking whether the two concepts are in any sense related. We also wanted to base our discussion on the ways in which both of these ideas describe the world which we experience round about us. If Teilhard de Chardin was right, then this becomes a question as to whether they are different ways in which different disciplines describe the same flaw in the universe. The Second Law of Thermodynamics is, of course, defined in any reputable textbook on physical science. What is meant by Original Sin varies from theologian to theologian and from person to person and its use in this book has therefore been defined carefully. It might be helpful if the church could get to grips with what it really means by Original Sin without simply resorting to quotations from the past, although this was, of course, the very issue which caused such trouble for Teilhard de Chardin. Nevertheless, it is an important issue and a process in which the present discussion might provide some help and which might also be helped by a wider understanding of the Second Law of Thermodynamics.

The clear answer to our question which has emerged from this study is that there are striking parallels between the Second Law of Thermodynamics and Original Sin and that they offer scientific and theological descriptions of the disorder which is present within the universe. In terms of the possible ways of describing the relationship between science and religion as outlined by Ian

Barbour, they are certainly not in conflict, nor do they describe mutually exclusive areas of life.[1] It is just possible that these two descriptions could be synthesized into a single united thesis, but that is beyond the scope of what we are trying to achieve and I believe that it would also be less than helpful. I am firmly of the belief that it is in the dialogue that truth emerges and if such a dialogue is to occur, then the church certainly needs to decide what is meant by Original Sin.

In his book *Proper Confidence*, Leslie Newbigin contrasts what he sees as the two dominant worldviews.[2] He states that the first of these sees ultimate reality as impersonal and beyond ourselves, and the second sees it as personal – contained within a story of which we are a part. We might think of the first as scientific and the second as religious. Newbigin makes the point that if we believe that truth lies beyond ourselves and is governed by ultimate principles, then we can predict the future. However, as part of the same point he also notes that if we believe that the truth is contained within a story and that this story is still being told, then we cannot predict the future in this way for the future has not yet been decided. Any certainty which we may claim to have rests on the faithfulness of the one who is telling the story.

From the perspective of the present work, this is the difference between looking at the world and seeing it on the one hand in terms of the Second Law of Thermodynamics and on the other hand in terms of Original Sin. These two descriptions may well be different ways of talking about the same phenomena and, within our current premise, they are both correct. However, the Second Law taken in isolation leads us to predict a future which is one of disorder and ultimate decay – if this is the whole story then we know the way in which the world will end. On the other hand, the unfinished story of Sin and salvation suggests that we are dependent upon the grace of God and His response to a creation in which things can go wrong – the future here involves trust, and the end is both unknown and ultimately more hopeful. These are two quite different ways of looking at the same physical observations of the universe in which we live.

Newbigin goes on to make a second point about his two worldviews. He sees the first worldview as being about grasping concepts (he calls it a 'vision') and then putting them into practice, whilst the second worldview is about a personal relationship based on experience. This is the distinction between *theoria* and *praxis*. He maintains that the way of faith is the way of relationship and praxis.

We might be tempted to once more see this distinction as akin to that between science and religion. However, this time the distinction breaks down. Most scientific research (as distinct from our knowledge of science) is actually based, in some way, upon experiment or praxis, what John Polkinghorne has termed 'bottom-up theology'. Theories are developed from observations and, as we have already noted in Chapter 2, the scientist is part of a relationship and cannot exist in isolation from that which he is examining. Unfortunately, despite its also supposedly being about relationships and experience, much so-called religion actually tends to be based not on a loving relationship but upon rules and regulations and the application of these within daily life. In their everyday operation religion and science can actually work in precisely the opposite way to that which we might expect. It is certainly incorrect to claim that they have their own specific ways of working which in no sense overlap with each other. Indeed, we might also want to make some dispute with Newbigin's first claim. Whilst I am quite sure that he did not wish to claim that we can currently predict the future with certainty, he implies that this is clearly possible in principle. Yet this claim relies on an understanding of the universe which is both realist and reductionist. As we have seen in Chapter 2 this is a claim which is, at its best, quite dubious.

In his book, *Grounds for Reasonable Belief*, Russell Stannard (who is both a former professor of experimental physics and a licensed Reader in the Church of England) devotes the last two chapters to an examination of the similarities between religion and science and an examination of the areas where they remain distinct.[3] In examining the similarities, he first notes that both deal with a bewildering array of events and seek to discover some form of order and meaning from the data which describes these events. However, as we have seen already, neither of the two fields does this in a purely objective manner. Both science and religion base their ordering of the data upon presuppositions about the form of the underlying principles. In the one case these are the basic 'laws of science' and in the other they are the basic doctrines of the religion concerned. The relationship between these two fields is that discussed in Chapter 2. Within our present context, the Second Law of Thermodynamics and the doctrine of Original Sin would appear to be the corresponding results obtained by science and Christian religion when they consider that part of the data which relates to order, decay and death.

The second similarity noted by Stannard is that because both science and religion operate within their own guiding frameworks, they can easily become blinkered to information and experience which does not conform to their expectations. The period of the Reformation demonstrates this for both science and the Christian church. An example within science concerns the orbiting of the earth around the sun, and an example within the church would be the understanding of doctrines of salvation. In the former case religion had erroneously become part of the scientific picture and tried to dictate that it was actually the sun which revolves around the earth, whilst in the latter case the theological issue was confused and driven by civil politics.[4] The risk in the present context is that both science and Christianity may consider the parallels which we have noted between Sin and the Second Law and then respond with an answer of 'so what?'

rather than asking what might be learned from such dialogue.

Nevertheless, Stannard notes a third similarity, namely that in both fields the evidence for change is sometimes so overwhelming that a paradigm shift is needed. Scientific examples include the rotation of the earth around the sun, the evidence for subatomic particles or the idea that particles can be described as waves. In each case the old scientific picture broke down and a new one had to emerge. In theology, the appearance, life and death of Jesus of Nazareth led to the emergence of the Christian faith from Judaism and, for many of those who knew or encountered Jesus, the old religious worldview no longer described their experience.

Once such turning points have been reached the question becomes one of how to test the new knowledge. One philosophical approach was to demand proof – the so-called verification principle which we examined in Chapter 2. However, as we noted, this has fallen into disrepute both in science and philosophy – a fact which is ignored by those who demand or produce proofs within theology. The fact that the principle itself fails its own test of truth (nothing can be accepted until it is proven true) is little appreciated in a world which demands facts even when they do not exist. A more recent idea is that all things are true until they are falsified and that all truth claims must be open to falsification. This too poses problems, both of the kind which doubt how some things could ever be falsified and also because evidence is routinely discarded in the belief that further development will show that this rejection of data was the correct way in which to proceed.

As a fourth similarity, Stannard noted that science and religion are both the activities of a community. This is not simply to state that they both involve groups and people working together in cooperation, not least because both science and religion contain quite obvious exceptions to this particular interpretation. It is rather to state that the framework of what is correct is decided by the community and that paradigm shifts are similarly the result of the collective consciousness of the community. A scientist who introduces a set of radically new ideas will experience stiff opposition, no matter how rigorous his methodology or how true his theory or results later turn out to be. The work of Charles Darwin which we noted in Chapter 2 is a good example of this. It is usually forgotten that Darwin experienced more opposition from the scientific community than he did from the church, largely because he disturbed the vested interests of many leading amateur scientists of the day. The way in which paradigm shifts are generated by the community is another example of bottom-up thinking. If enough people believe something and can act according to their beliefs then they are able to rewrite the rules.

Fifthly, both theological development and scientific discovery build on what has gone before, even in the case when a paradigm shift occurs. Jesus Himself relied heavily upon the understanding and experience of the Jewish religion. Without this understanding His mission would have been impossible or would have needed to take a very different form. The present work seeks to build on the understanding of both scientific and Christian communities, albeit that its intended audience is more Christian than scientific. Indeed, the scientific community might not be in the slightest bit interested to discover that, in their terms, Original Sin could be a manifestation of the Second Law of Thermodynamics or vice versa.

Sixthly, the idea of objectivity has to be ruled out in both fields. Modern physics has destroyed the myth of scientific objectivity, even if the concept of such destruction has not caught on in popular belief. Both science and religion rely on the relationship between the practitioner and that with which he or she is concerned.

Seventhly, both science and religion stretch language, using a wide range of metaphors and models in order to describe the indescribable and to mean things which are beyond any literal meaning which the words might already have. In both fields it is always important to ask the question which begins, 'What do we/you mean by ...?'[5]

Finally, both science and religion are quite confident in dealing with the raw data which falls within their remit, but less certain in going beyond that remit in order to consider the possible implications of the questions which lie behind their understanding. Physicists are just as entrenched in their speculations as are the authors of books on the various and indeed the same religious faiths. To contrast the so-called 'hard facts' of science with the 'speculation' of faith is not to compare like with like. Both science and theology are good at dealing with the hard facts of their own field of expertise and both contain a mixture of divergent dogmatic certitude and the questioning of the unknown when they move beyond these core beliefs. The present work has hopefully compared like with like and shown that the parallels are indeed there.

However, it is important that we do not understand this demonstration to mean that we have produced a synthesis of the two disciplines. Stannard has also observed notable dissimilarities between the two, the most important of which is surely that science studies an impersonal object whereas theology in general and Christianity in particular engages with a personal 'object' (for want of a better term) with whom it is possible to have a genuine relationship. In science the principal focus which is generated within the 'I–it' relationship is determined by the wishes of the 'I', whereas in theology the 'I–God' dialogue should be much more focused on the wishes and demands of 'God'. This distinction is very important, especially as the other distinctions put forward by Stannard are rather more hazy, such as the ways in which he contrasts the use of metaphor in the two fields and the accessibility of the raw data. However, it is when he moves on to consider the idea of 'personal involvement' that his distinction becomes stretched to breaking point. He writes, 'What marks out the religious way of life from other human activities like the pursuit of science, is that it involves a *total* commitment.'[6] It is an easily observed fact that for many members of the church, such total commitment is simply not present in their religious faith, whereas for some practitioners of science, their scientific research has indeed moved to the point where it dominates their whole life and intellectual standpoint. Perhaps the sociological and psychological similarities between science and the Christian faith are rather more profound than we might dare to think.

In the context of Stannard's observations, it is notable that in exploring the parallels which may exist between Original Sin and the Second Law of Thermodynamics, we have discovered ways in which these two apparently different concepts have a number of profound similarities. Moreover, the Second Law of Thermodynamics and Original Sin as defined here both appear to describe the world as it is; indeed they both appear to describe the same aspects of the world which we experience in our daily lives. Whether this correspondence goes deeper and actually amounts to a common underlying identity is an issue which has not been resolved. To answer this question in the affirmative would be to make a definite claim about the relationship between science and religion. It would amount to a statement that the integration of the two disciplines could be humanly possible. This is a claim which is beyond both the scope and the intention of the present work. Given the mystery of God it is unclear whether such a claim would be useful even if it were to be the case. In the manner of one of my former chemistry lecturers, this issue is perhaps best left as an exercise for the individual.

Yet it is remarkable how the early Church Fathers, writing in a pre-scientific age, nevertheless managed to prefigure some of the issues which would later emerge in the dialogue between science and theology. As an example, Russell Stannard has noted how Augustine of Hippo both discussed the fact that it is meaningless to speak of a time before creation, because time was not, and how he also noted that intelligent life had developed from 'germs'. We end our present discussion with a quotation from Augustine of Hippo and we shall then conclude our study with a story – or rather with a myth which has something of a familiar ring to it.

Brethren, do our years last? They slip away day by day. Those which were, no longer are; those to come are not yet here. The former are past, the latter will come, only to pass away in their turn. Today exists only in the moment in which we speak. Its first hours have passed, the remainder do not yet exist; they will come, but only to fall into nothingness ... Nothing contains consistency in itself. The body does not process being: it has no permanence. It changes with age, it changes with time and place, it changes with illness and accident. The stars have as little consistency; they change in hidden ways, they go whirling through space ... They are not steady, they do not possess being. Nor is the human heart any more constant. How many thoughts disturb it, how many ambitions! How many pleasures draw it this way and that, tearing it apart! The human spirit itself, although endowed with reason, changes; it does not process being. It wills and does not will; it knows and it does not know; it remembers and forgets. No one has even himself the unity of being ... After so many sufferings, diseases, troubles and pains, let us return humbly to that One Being. Let us enter into that City whose inhabitants share in being itself.[7]

6.2 The Tale of Three Gardens: A Myth

Once upon a time [although time has no relevance in this section of the myth], there was a beautiful garden in which lived a woman and a man. In the garden there were also two trees, one known as the tree of everlasting life and the other as the tree of the knowledge of good and evil. It wasn't that the man and the woman could read the labels attached to the trees; they just knew that this was what they were called. Both of the trees bore beautiful fruit, and the man and the woman often wondered if this fruit would be good to eat.

One day the man and the woman could resist no longer and so it was that they decided to eat some of the fruit from one of the trees. The first tree they came across was the tree of everlasting life. They picked the fruit and bit into it and no sooner had they done so than the tree of the knowledge of good and evil disappeared.

As the centuries went by, so the man and the woman began to get bored with the fruit of the tree of everlasting life, and indeed, they became bored with the garden altogether. Although they had nothing to complain about, life seemed to have a certain sameness about it – although, as they never had any concept of today or of tomorrow by which they could judge their existence, they could never know how repetitive life was nor how tedious it would appear if it could be viewed from the outside. If they had been able to judge their lives in this way, then they would have wanted to die, but that was also a concept of which they had no knowledge; it was an experience of which they had no prospect, for nothing in the garden ever died. They are still there today – just the two of them. They still live in the garden and they still eat the fruit of the tree of everlasting life and they always will, for ever and ever. However, they will never remark upon or see any significance whatsoever in the fact that they are both completely naked.

Once upon a time [and this time we really mean it] there was another beautiful garden, in which lived a woman and a man. In this garden there were also two trees, one the tree of everlasting life and the other the tree of the knowledge of good and evil. Once again, it wasn't that the man and the woman could read the labels on the trees; they just knew what they were called. Again, just as in the first garden, both trees bore beautiful fruit, and the man and the woman often wondered if this fruit would be good to eat.

One day the woman and the man decided that it would be good to eat some of the fruit from one of the trees. In this garden, however, the first tree they came across was the tree of the knowledge of good and evil. They picked the fruit and bit into it, but no sooner had they done so, than the tree of everlasting life disappeared. They also realized, to their immense interest and fascination, that neither of them was wearing any clothing. However, they were also both worried in case anyone came along and saw them naked (not that anyone ever had – indeed there was no-one else in the garden) and as it also felt a bit cold, they made some garments and put them on.

Of course, now having an interest in such things, they proceeded to have children, as did their children and their children after them, until the whole place got rather crowded; not that the man and the woman knew anything about it, for they had both long since died. Indeed, most people wished the man and woman had eaten the fruit of the tree of life rather than the tree of the knowledge of good and evil so that no-one ever had to suffer or to die. Their children had long argued about who to blame for their parents' death and although they felt it was probably Mother's fault, because that was how society operated, they decided to blame a nearby serpent instead. They did this for the usual reasons, partly because they did not like the serpent and partly because it could not answer back. Also, since their parents had never discussed the matter with them, they could only imagine what God's reaction had been when their parents had first noticed their lack of clothing. Indeed, it was rumored that as a result of His displeasure God had thrown them out of the garden.

The strange thing was that although most people knew that

the tree in the center of the garden was the tree of the knowledge of good and evil, there were also those who said that there was no such thing as evil, nor was there even a garden, although strangely these were also the same people who could not explain why everyone had to die and who always complained whenever anything went wrong. Another strange thing was that although most people knew that the tree in the center of the garden was the tree of the knowledge of good and evil, the label on it said something quite different. The label actually stated that it was the tree of increasing disorder in the universe, which the people interpreted as meaning that they were able to make choices about their lives. They also felt that this freedom to choose was in some way connected with the inevitability of suffering and death. However, what no-one knew, despite the presence of many rumors, was that beyond death there was a new life in a third garden which had both everlasting life and free choices, and that this unseen garden was only possible because within their present garden grew the tree of increasing disorder within the universe; a tree which some people still knew as the tree of the knowledge of good and evil.

Notes

Chapter 1 Introduction

1   Bent (1965), p.28.

2   Genesis chapter 3 verses 6–7, 22.

3   See, for example, pp.135–136 of Speaight (1967).

4   Speaight (1967), pp.192ff.

5   Holloway (1994), pp.74f.

6   For example, Polkinghorne (1996), vii.

7   Polkinghorne (1994), p.15. For a detailed discussion of Sin see Pannenberg (1994), section 8.3, pp.231–265.

8   Polkinghorne (1991), p.99.

9   Barr (1992), pp.4ff.

10 Pannenberg (1994), p.245.

11 Tillich (1978), pp.39ff. According to Tillich, 'essence' is the ideal state and 'existence' that which actually occurs in practice.

12 Tillich (1978), pp.46f.

13 Pannenberg (1994), pp.245f.

14 Wright (1992), p.133.

15 Although this is the original form of the law, Einstein's development of his Special Theory of Relativity, which shows that mass and energy are interchangeable, means that it is more strictly correct to say that mass-energy can neither be created nor destroyed.

16 There is nothing particularly unique about this expression of the Second Law although it should be noted that this particular wording is taken from Smith (1977), p.21.

17 Again this formulation of the Second Law is not unique but the wording is taken from Peacocke (1993), p.52.

18 This is discussed in more detail in section 3.1.

19 Such quantities which always have the same value under particular physical conditions are known as 'state functions'.

Other examples include the internal energy of a substance and the free energy of a substance. Both of these quantities will be discussed further in Chapter 3.

20 See Peacocke (1993), pp.55–61.

21 Peacocke (1993), pp.61–69, especially p.65.

22 The speed in each case is measured relative to the normal lifespan of the organism involved.

23 This claim itself says something about the presuppositions present in the present study. In making the statement I am effectively arguing against the possibility of being wholly objective and therefore rejecting a positivist approach to the world. See further, section 2.2 in the present work and also Hough (2000).

24 Wright (1992), pp.131–134.

25 Wright (1992), p.132.

Chapter 2 The Relationship between Science and Theology

1 A view which is epitomized in the various writings of Richard Dawkins.

2 Peacocke (1993), viii.

3 The fact that Newton held Unitarian beliefs rather than Trinitarian ones does nothing to annul this assertion.

4 The opposition to Darwin came largely from the dying breed of 'gentleman scientist', who engaged in scientific research as a hobby funded from his own means. Darwin represented the new breed of professional scientist which threatened to change the balance of power in scientific investigations. For an excellent discussion of Darwin's work, more recent developments and its implication both for theology and the present day, see Peters and Hewlett (2008).

5 Raven (1943), p.10.

6 These lectures were published in 1955; see Coulson (1955). Their enduring significance in the present day has been

discussed by Hough (2006).

7   A good example of this suspicion of science concerns the common assumption that chemicals are dangerous, a view which fails to take note of the fact that we ourselves are made entirely of chemicals as is everything which we eat, see, smell, touch or hear.

8   Raven (1943), pp.33ff. See also Hough (1997), pp.24–25.

9   The whole issue of the misrepresentation of the science and religion debate in popular opinion as well as in apparently serious accounts has been discussed by Brooke and Cantor (1998); see also Peters and Hewlett (2008).

10 Raven (1943), pp.36ff; Peacocke (1993), p.4; Brooke and Cantor (1998), pp.161–166.

11 See, for example, Peacocke (1993), p.20.

12 Barbour (1990), pp.3ff. See also Barbour (1992).

13 Brooke and Cantor (1998) provide a good description of such scriptural geology.

14 For example, Brooke and Cantor (1998), pp.106–132; Southgate et al. (1999), pp.27–32.

15 Barbour (1990), pp.23ff.

16 For a discussion of a number of aspects of panentheism and process theology, including some of their problems and the way in which their alleged insights are already present within traditional Christian doctrine, see Hough (1997).

17 Stannard (1989), pp.310ff.

18 It could be argued that modern science contains and demonstrates a number of deviations from this premise, especially if the statement is intended as an absolute. However, the development of classical science prior to the twentieth century knew nothing of such considerations and it is this development in which we are interested.

19 This latter point is discussed by Von Rad (1965), pp.336ff.

20 The importance of the Greek influence here is often ignored and scientific development is attributed solely to the Judeo-

Christian worldview. It should be remembered that this worldview was heavily influenced by Greek culture.

21 Polkinghorne (2004), pp.11–31.

22 See, for example, Davies (1990).

23 Polkinghorne (2004), p.26.

24 This issue has been discussed by Brooke and Cantor (1998); see pp.275f.

25 See Hough (2006). Although the concept already existed, it appears to have been Coulson who coined the actual phrase 'the God of the gaps'.

26 Stannard (1989), p.4.

27 Stannard (1989), pp.7–14; pp.325f.

28 Wright (1992), p.98.

29 Polkinghorne (1994), p.31.

30 See Stannard (1989), pp.1–2. Having met such a person it would presumably be quite consistent for us to decide that they themselves did not exist and therefore to ignore them!

31 This approach has been applied explicitly to the Christological quest by Hough (2000).

32 Peacocke (1993), pp.19–20.

33 Barbour (1990), pp.31–41. A similar account is given by Wright (1992), pp.99ff. He combines the essence of Barbour's third and fourth points within a single point and then applies the resulting criteria both to Jesus and to Paul.

34 Since the 1980s there has been something of a renaissance in studies of the doctrine of the Trinity. This is now starting to correct the lip-service which had been paid to it by the church, especially in popular belief and in relating its importance and significance to everyday life. Examples of such discussions occur in Moltmann (1981), (1991), Torrance (1996), Cunningham (1998) and Hough (1997), especially ch.6.

35 Polkinghorne (1994), p.47. A 'high-level' theory is one which encompasses a great deal of data and which can draw

together a number of different areas of study.

36   See the discussion in Brooke and Cantor (1998), ch.7, pp.207–243. The authors consider the premise and the way it has been presented, before providing a detailed discussion as to why the premise is false.

37   An example of the way in which these claims apply to Christology has been provided by Hough (2000) who discusses critical realism and the quest for knowledge of Jesus.

38   Discussed in Brooke and Cantor (1998), pp.83ff.

39   See, for example, Barbour (1990), pp.60ff and Polkinghorne (1994), pp.47ff.

40   The details of the way in which the simple relationship which works well under normal conditions has to be modified, then replaced altogether as conditions become more extreme, can be found in any textbook of physical chemistry.

41   See, for example, Southgate et al. (1999), pp.153–163.

42   Polkinghorne (1994), pp.28–29. See also Peacocke (1993), pp.39–41 and Barbour (1990), pp.109ff.

43   Polkinghorne (1991), pp.44f.

44   A good example of such a desire appeared in the journal *Chemistry in Britain* during 1993. Here, a scientific article on 'Self-assembling organic systems', began with the claim that reductionism plays too great a part in chemistry. Religious belief was not mentioned in the article. The article drew a response which was published in the letters column. The author of this response stated that readers should be aware that the approach in the earlier article was a wedge aimed to open gaps into which some thinkers would insert their concept of God. The editorial decision to publish this letter must surely be open to criticism.

45   See Barbour (1990), p.101.

Chapter 3 Sin and the Second Law

1   We should nevertheless recall James Barr's observation that in early Jewish tradition the discussion about human mortality did not become complicated by reference to Sin, but focused on the cause of mortality as explained in the expulsion of Adam and Eve from the Garden of Eden. Barr claims that the story contained in Genesis chapters 2 and 3 was originally about mortality and not about Sin or sins. See Barr (1992).

2   Romans chapter 8 verse 21.

3   Bent (1965), p.3.

4   If ΔH is the change in heat, T the temperature in Kelvin and ΔS the change in entropy, then in a purely physical change such as freezing and melting, the disorder produced by a given amount of heat is described by: $\Delta H = -T\Delta S$ or $\Delta S = -\Delta H/T$.

5   Such a recovery of energy rarely happens in practice and the lost heat can be seen in the steam which rises from the cooling towers of many power stations. Unfortunately, it is usually cheaper to burn more coal and thereby produce both additional pollution and more waste heat, than it is to recover some of the waste heat in a form which can be put to use.

6   For the mathematically minded, the formula for calculating the entropy of a system is that $S = k.\ln W$, that is, that the entropy (S) is equal to the Boltzmann constant (k) multiplied by the natural logarithm of the number of ways of arranging the system.

7   It is important to remember that the universe operates on an interplay between law and chance and that in scientific terms it is this interplay which is creative. This is discussed, for example, in Peacocke (1993), pp.63ff and 72ff.

8   Stannard (1989), p.97.

9   See Peacocke (1993), pp.31–32.

10   See Chapter 4 for a discussion of the theories of the atonement.
11   See Barr (1992), ch.1.

Chapter 4 Atonement and the Second Law

1   See Pannenberg (1968), pp.38f.
2   Moltmann (1974), p.7.
3   A good readable discussion can be found in Stephen Sykes' book, *The Story of the Atonement*, Sykes (1997).
4   This has been discussed with great practical emphasis by C. FitzSimons Allison (1994), pp.119–137.
5   These ideas have been discussed in detail by many authors, notably Stott (1986).
6   A useful summary can be found in McGrath (1993), pp.106–109.
7   The English translation appeared in 1931.
8   Moltmann (1974), pp.219f.
9   Williams (1994), pp.89–94.
10   Romans chapter 8 verse 21.
11   Petersen (1995), p.83.
12   See Thornton (1963), p.113.
13   Fiddes (2000), p.178.
14   Lindars (1990), pp.81f.
15   For example, Moltmann (1981); Fiddes (1989), (2000).
16   Pannenberg (1994), p.399.
17   See Haffner (1995), pp.126ff.
18   These are all issues which I have discussed in Hough (1997).

Chapter 5 Doctrine and the Second Law

1   This issue is explored in many modern books on the Trinity, e.g. Moltmann (1981), (1991).
2   Pannenberg (1994), p.319.
3   For a simple discussion, see Hough (1997), pp.91ff.
4   See Hough (2000).

5   Athanasius, *De Incarnatione*.

6   Pannenberg (1994), p.306.

7   Whether or not Jesus did commit such misdeeds is a separate issue; see later in the text.

8   Barth used the two German words for 'history' – *Historie* and *Geschichte* – quite differently. According to Barth, *Historie* is the usual course of human events as viewed on earth, whilst *Geschichte* is the breaking in of divine action 'from above'.

9   Moltmann (1974), pp.178f.

10   Lindars (1990), pp.81–82.

11   See Lash (1988), p.19.

12   The classic survey of these studies up to the end of the nineteenth century is that provided by Schweitzer (1906, 1996).

13   Fiddes (1989).

14   Torrance (1976).

15   The word 'creation' is used here simply to imply that God's purpose lay behind the universe coming into existence.

16   For example, Hough (1997), ch.6.

17   For further discussion see Hough (1997), ch.3.

18   See, for example, Lovelock (1979).

19   A good review of the argument can be found in Brooke and Cantor (1998).

20   Athanasius, *De Incarnatione*, ch.6.

21   See Peacocke (1993), pp.49–51.

22   Polkinghorne (1991), pp.99–100; (1996), p.13.

23   Clement (1993), p.110.

24   Lash (1988), p.211.

25   Lash quotes Buber on pp.203 and 204 of *Easter in Ordinary*, Lash (1988), but fails to provide a reference. However, the context indicates that these are quotations from Buber (1970).

Chapter 6 Where Do We Go From Here?

1 Barbour (1990), pp.3ff; see also section 2.2 in the present work.
2 Newbigin (1995), p.13f.
3 Stannard (1989). Chapter 19 deals with the similarities and Chapter 20 with the distinctions.
4 See Lohse (1986), ch.3.
5 For a discussion on the use of models and metaphors see Soskice (1985), or for a shorter account, Hough (1997), ch.6.
6 Stannard (1989), p.317, his italics.
7 Augustine of Hippo commentary on Psalm 121 verse 6, quoted in Clement (1998).

Bibliography

Allison, C.F. *The Cruelty of Heresy: An Affirmation of Christian Orthodoxy*, SPCK / Morehouse, 1994.

Athanasius *Contra Gentes and De Incarnatione*, edited and translated by R.W. Thomson, Oxford Early Christian Texts, OUP, 1971 or *St Athanasius on the Incarnation*, Mowbray, 1953, reissued by Create-Space, 2003.

Aulen, G. *Christus Victor*, English edition, SPCK, 1953, reissued by Wipf & Stock, 2003.

Barbour, I.G. *Religion in an Age of Science*, SCM / HarperOne, 1990.

Barbour, I.G. *Ethics in an Age of Technology*, SCM / HarperOne, 1992.

Barr, J. *The Garden of Eden and the Hope of Immortality*, SCM, 1992 / Fortress Press, 1993.

Bent, H.A. *The Second Law: An Introduction to Classical and Statistical Thermodynamics*, Oxford University Press, 1965.

Brooke, J. and Cantor, C. *Reconstructing Nature: The Engagement of Science and Religion*, T&T Clark, 1998 / Oxford University Press, 2000.

Buber, M. *I and Thou*, English translation, T&T Clark, 1970, reissued by Hesperides Press, 2008.

Clement, O. *The Roots of Christian Mysticism*, English translation, New City, 1998.

Coulson, C.A. *Science and Christian Belief*, Oxford University Press, 1955 / Chapel Hill, Collins, 1958.

Cunningham, D.S. *These Three are One: The Practice of Trinitarian Theology*, Blackwell / Wiley-Blackwell, 1998.

Davies, P. *God and the New Physics*, Penguin, 1990.

Fiddes, P.S. *Past Event and Present Salvation: The Christian Idea of Atonement*, Darton, Longman and Todd / Westminster John Knox Press, 1989.

Fiddes, P.S. *Participating in God: A Pastoral Doctrine of The Trinity*, Darton, Longman and Todd, 2000 / Westminster John Knox Press, 2001.

Haffner, P. *Mystery of Creation*, Gracewing/Fowler Wright, 1995.

Holloway, R. *The Stranger in the Wings: Affirming Faith in the God of Surprises*, SPCK, 1994.

Hough, A.M. *God is not 'Green': A Re-examination of Eco-Theology*, Gracewing/Fowler Wright, 1997.

Hough, A.M. 'On Every Street: Critically Real Christology', *Modern Believing*, pp.14–20, July 2000.

Hough, A.M. 'Not a Gap in Sight: Fifty Years of Charles Coulson's Science and Christian Belief', *Theology*, pp. 21–27, January/February 2006.

Lash, N. *Easter in Ordinary: Reflections on Human Experience and the Knowledge of God*, SCM, 1988 / University of Notre Dame, 1990.

Lindars, B. *John: New Testament Study Guide*, Sheffield Academic Press, 1990.

Lohse, B. *Martin Luther: An Introduction to His Life and Work*, T&T Clark, 1986 / Augsburg-Fortress Press, 2000.

Lovelock, J. *Gaia: A New Look at Life on Earth*, Oxford University Press, 1979.

McGrath, A.E. *Reformation Thought: An Introduction*, 2nd edn, Blackwell / Wiley-Blackwell, 1993.

McGrath, A.E. *The Order of Things: Explorations in Scientific Theology*, Blackwell / Wiley-Blackwell, 2006.

Moltmann, J. *The Crucified God*, English translation, SCM, 1974.

Moltmann, J. *The Trinity and the Kingdom of God*, English translation, SCM / Harper & Row, 1981.

Moltmann, J. *History and the Triune God*, English translation, SCM, 1991 / Crossroad, 1992.

Moltmann, J. *Science and Wisdom*, English translation, SCM / Augsburg Fortress Press, 2003.

Newbigin, L. *Proper Confidence: Faith, Doubt and Certainty in*

Christian Discipleship, SPCK, 1995.

Pannenberg, W. *Jesus: God and Man*, English translation, SCM / Westminster John Knox Press, 1968.

Pannenberg, W. *Systematic Theology Volume 2*, English translation, T&T Clark / Eerdmans, 1994.

Peacocke, A.R. *Theology for a Scientific Age*, enlarged edition, SCM / Augsburg Fortress Press, 1993.

Peters, T. and Hewlett, M. *Theological and Scientific Commentary on Darwin's Origin of Species*, Abingdon, 2008.

Pettersen, A. *Athanasius*, Geoffrey Chapman, 1995.

Polkinghorne, J. *Reason and Reality*, SPCK / Trinity Press International, 1991.

Polkinghorne, J. *Science and Christian Belief - Theological reflections of a bottom-up thinker*, SPCK, 1994

Polkinghorne, J. *Serious Talk: Science and Religion in Dialogue*, SCM / Trinity Press International, 1996.

Polkinghorne, J. *Science and the Trinity: The Christian Encounter with Reality*, SPCK, 2004 / Yale University Press, 2006.

Raven, C. *Science, Religion and the Future*, Cambridge University Press, 1943, reissued by Mowbray, 1994 and Cambridge University Press, 2009.

Schweitzer, A. *The Quest for the Historical Jesus*, 1906, English translation, A&C Black, 1954, reissued by SCM, 1996.

Smith, E.B. *Basic Chemical Thermodynamics*, Oxford University Press, 1977.

Soskice, J.M. *Metaphor and Religious Language*, Oxford University Press, 1985.

Southgate, C. et al. *God, Humanity and the Cosmos: A Textbook in Science and Religion*, T&T Clark / Continuum, 1999.

Speaight, R. *Teilhard de Chardin: A Biography*, Collins, 1967.

Stannard, R. *Grounds for Reasonable Belief*, Scottish Academic Press, 1989.

Stott, J.R.W. *The Cross of Christ*, Inter-Varsity Press, 1986, reissued 2006.

Sykes, S. *The Story of the Atonement*, Darton, Longman and Todd, 1997.

Thornton, M. *English Spirituality*, SPCK, 1963; reissued by Cowley Publications, 1986.

Tillich, P. *Systematic Theology II*, University of Chicago Press, 1957, reissued by SCM, 1978.

Torrance, T. *Space, Time and Resurrection*, Oxford University Press, 1976 / Continuum 1998.

Torrance, T.F. *The Christian Doctrine of God: One Being Three Persons*, T&T Clark, 1996.

Von Rad, G. *Old Testament Theology II*, English edition, SCM / Harper & Row, 1965.

Williams, R. *Open to Judgement: Sermons and Addresses*, Darton, Longman and Todd, 1994.

Wright, N.T. *The New Testament and the People of God*, SPCK / Augsburg Fortress Press, 1992.

BOOKS

O is a symbol of the world, of oneness and unity. In different cultures it also means the "eye," symbolizing knowledge and insight. We aim to publish books that are accessible, constructive and that challenge accepted opinion, both that of academia and the "moral majority."

Our books are available in all good English language bookstores worldwide. If you don't see the book on the shelves ask the bookstore to order it for you, quoting the ISBN number and title. Alternatively you can order online (all major online retail sites carry our titles) or contact the distributor in the relevant country, listed on the copyright page.

See our website www.o-books.net for a full list of over 500 titles, growing by 100 a year.

And tune in to myspiritradio.com for our book review radio show, hosted by June-Elleni Laine, where you can listen to the authors discussing their books.